ROUGH DOG PRESS

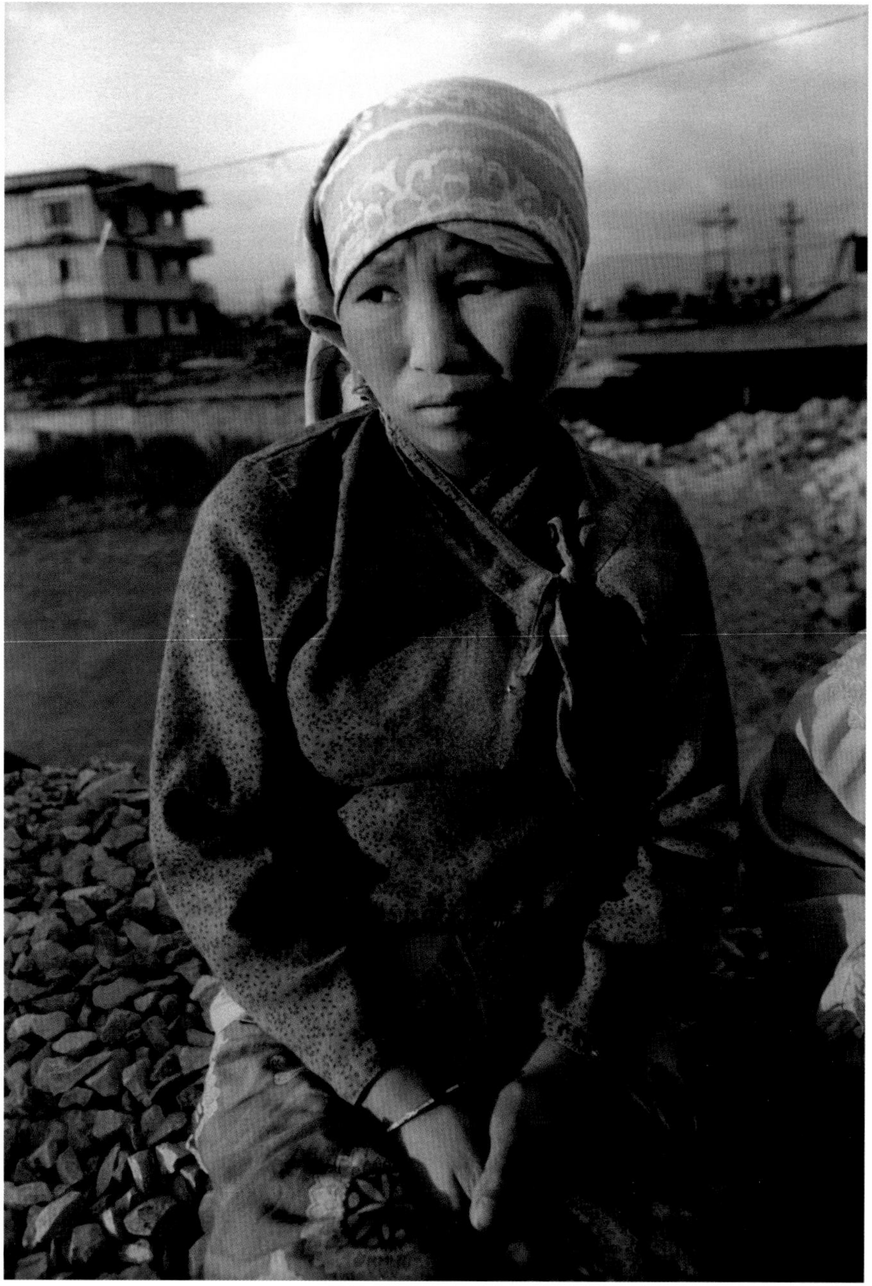

STONEFACTORY

OLOF JARLBRO

ROUGH DOG PRESS

In the outskirts of Kathmandu is Koteshwor, a big dusty crossroad between Kathmandu and Bhaktapur. Because of the heavy traffic of trucks and buses, the whole area has become a big truck stop with auto mechanics, street vendors and fast-food stalls. This area is not described in any travel guides. Next to Koteshwor flows the river Jadibuti and on each side of the river lies two small stonemills. The workers in the stone factories live in small metal shacks located on the grounds of the factory. They crush big blocks of stones to grit for construction. The daily wages various from 70 to 150 NRP, which equals 0.60 to 1.40 €. The factory normally runs from dawn till dusk. The dusty conditions endanger the health of the workers: many of them suffer from incurable asthma, which is constantly getting worse and hinders their ability to make a living. The workers' children normally become employees when they are old enough to carry stones.

Photographs in this book were made at various times between 2002-2008.

Koteshwor est situé dans la périphérie de Katmandou. C`est un grand carrefour poussiéreux entre Katmandou et Bhaktapur. En raison d`une circulation dense, l'ensemble de la zone est devenue un gros camion arrêté à la mécanique automobile, pleine de vendeurs dans les rues et des étals de fast-food. Ce domaine n'est pas décrit dans les guides de voyage. Près de Koteshwor se situe la rivière Jadibuti. Ainsi de chaque côté de la rivière se trouve deux petites usines de pierre. Les travailleurs dans les usines de pierre vivent dans des petites cabanes en métal situées sur le terrain de l'usine. Ils écrasent de grands blocs de pierres au grain de construction. Les salaires journaliers sont entre 70 et 150 NRP, l`équivalent de 0,60 et 1,40 €. L'usine fonctionne normalement de l'aube au crépuscule. Les conditions poussiéreux mettent en danger la santé des travailleurs: un grand nombre d'entre eux souffrent de l'asthme incurable, qui ne cesse de s'aggraver et entraver leur capacité à gagner leur vie. En général, les enfants des travailleurs sont les futures employés des usines, quand ils deviennent assez grands pour transporter les pierres.

Les photographies de ce livre ont été prises dans de différents moments entre 2002-2008.

Na okraji Kathmandu je Koteshwor, velká prašná křižovatka mezi Kathmandu a Bhaktapurem. Z důvodu hustého provozu nákladních automobilů a autobusů, se celá oblast stala obrovskou dopravní arterií s automechniky, pouličními prodejci a Fast-food stánky. Tato oblast není popsáná v žádném z cestovních průvodců. V sousedství s Koteshorem na řece Jadibuti se nacházejí dve malé továrny (kamenné mlýny). Dělníci žijí v malých kovovych chatrčích v přízemí továrny. Drtí velké bloky kamenů na štěrk pro stavbu. Denní výdělek se pohybuje v rozmezí 70 - 150 nepálských rupií, což je v přepočtu asi 1 - 1,5 Euro. Prašné podmínky ohrožují zdraví dělníků: mnoho z nich trpí nevyléčitelným astma, které se neustále zhoršuje a brání jim vydělat na živobytí. Jakmile jsou jejich děti dost staré a silné, aby unesly kámen, obvykle se stavají zaměstnanci továrny.

Fotografie v této knize byly pořizeny v období 2002-2008.

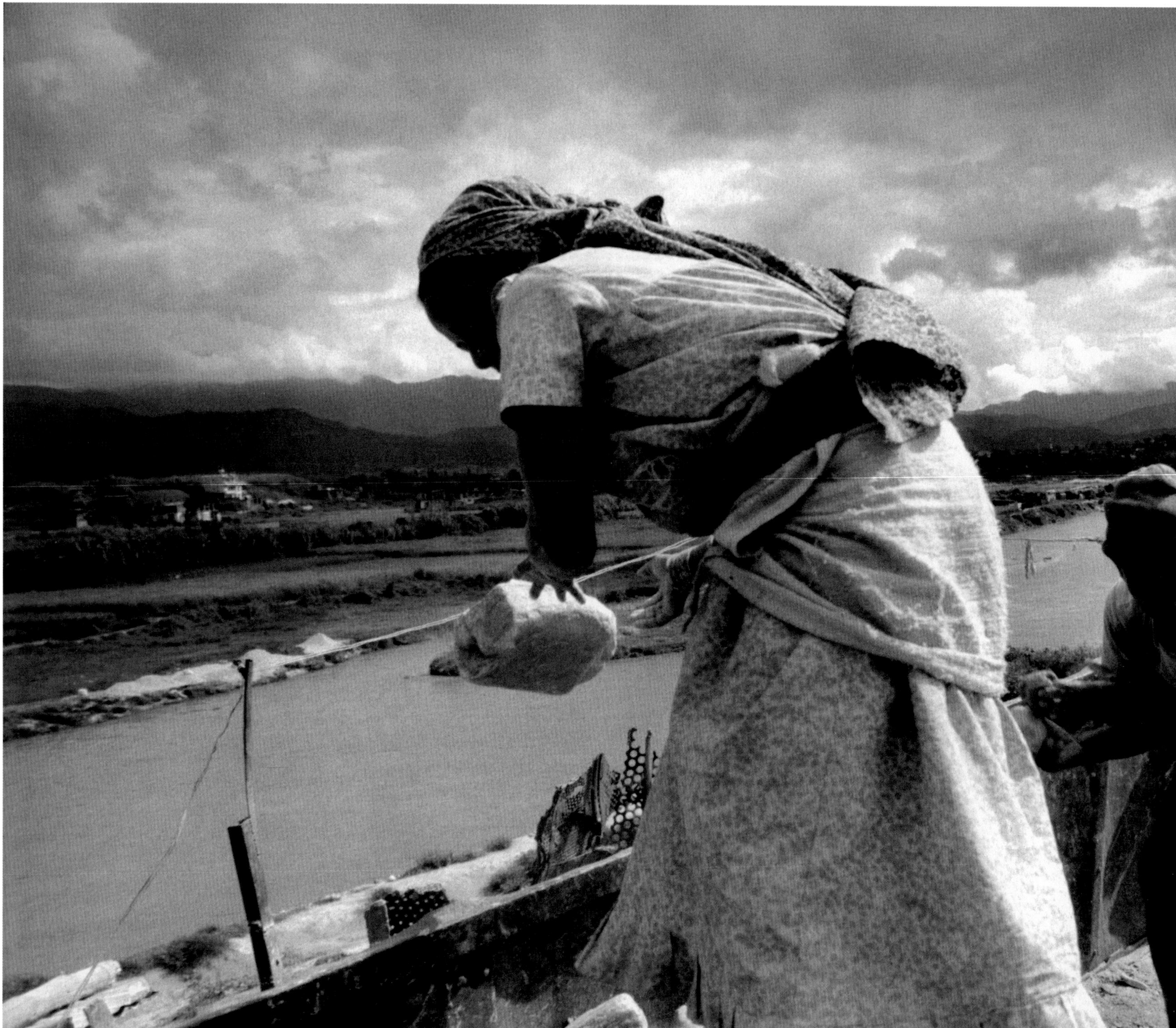

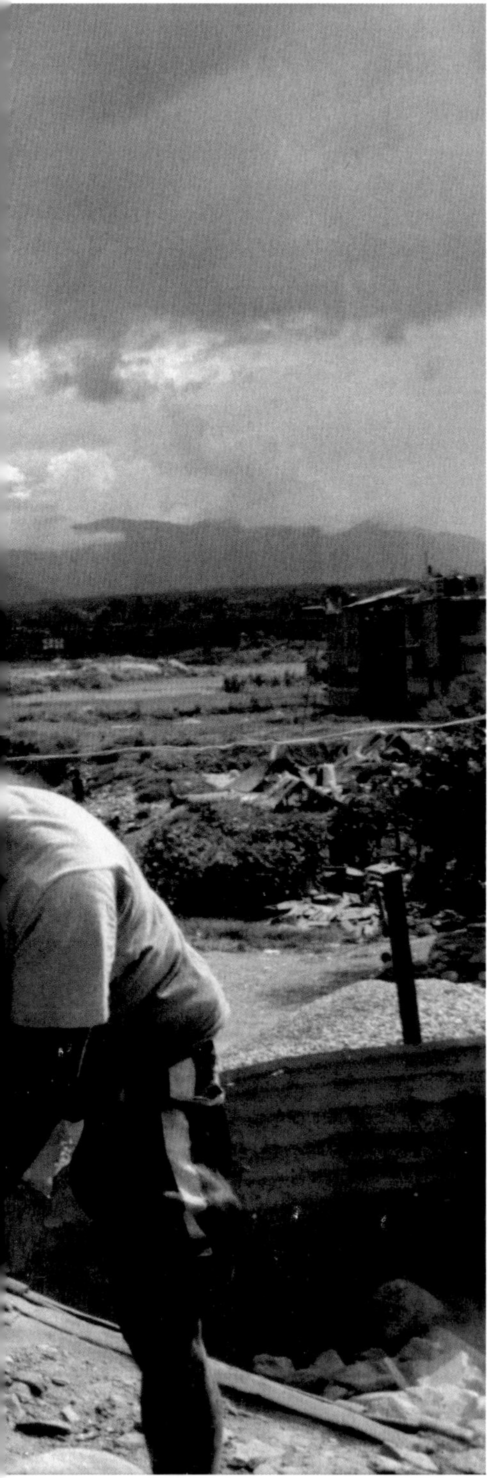

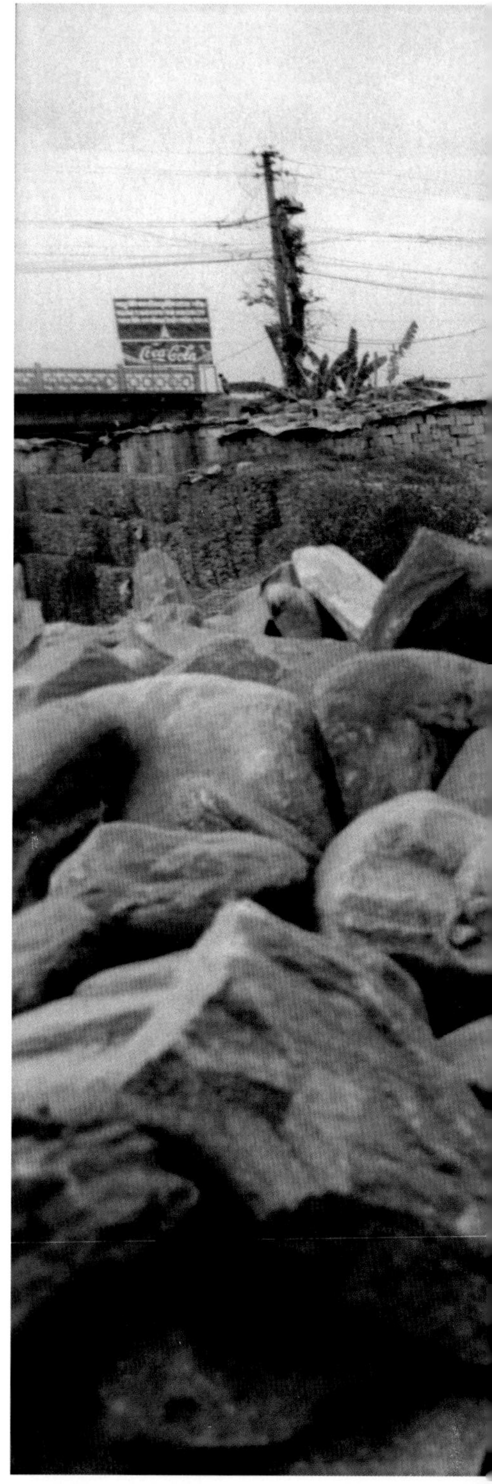
Coca-Cola

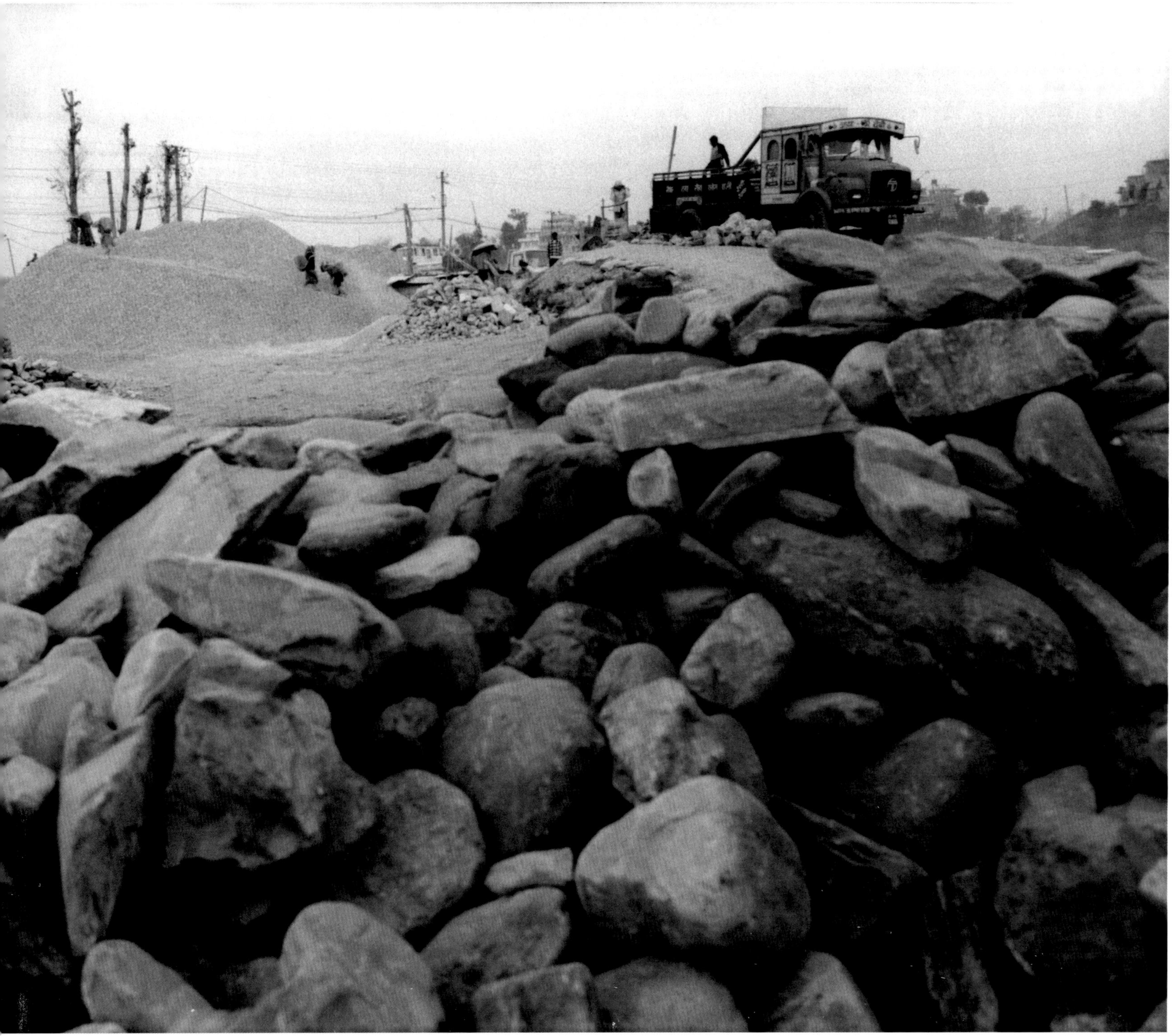

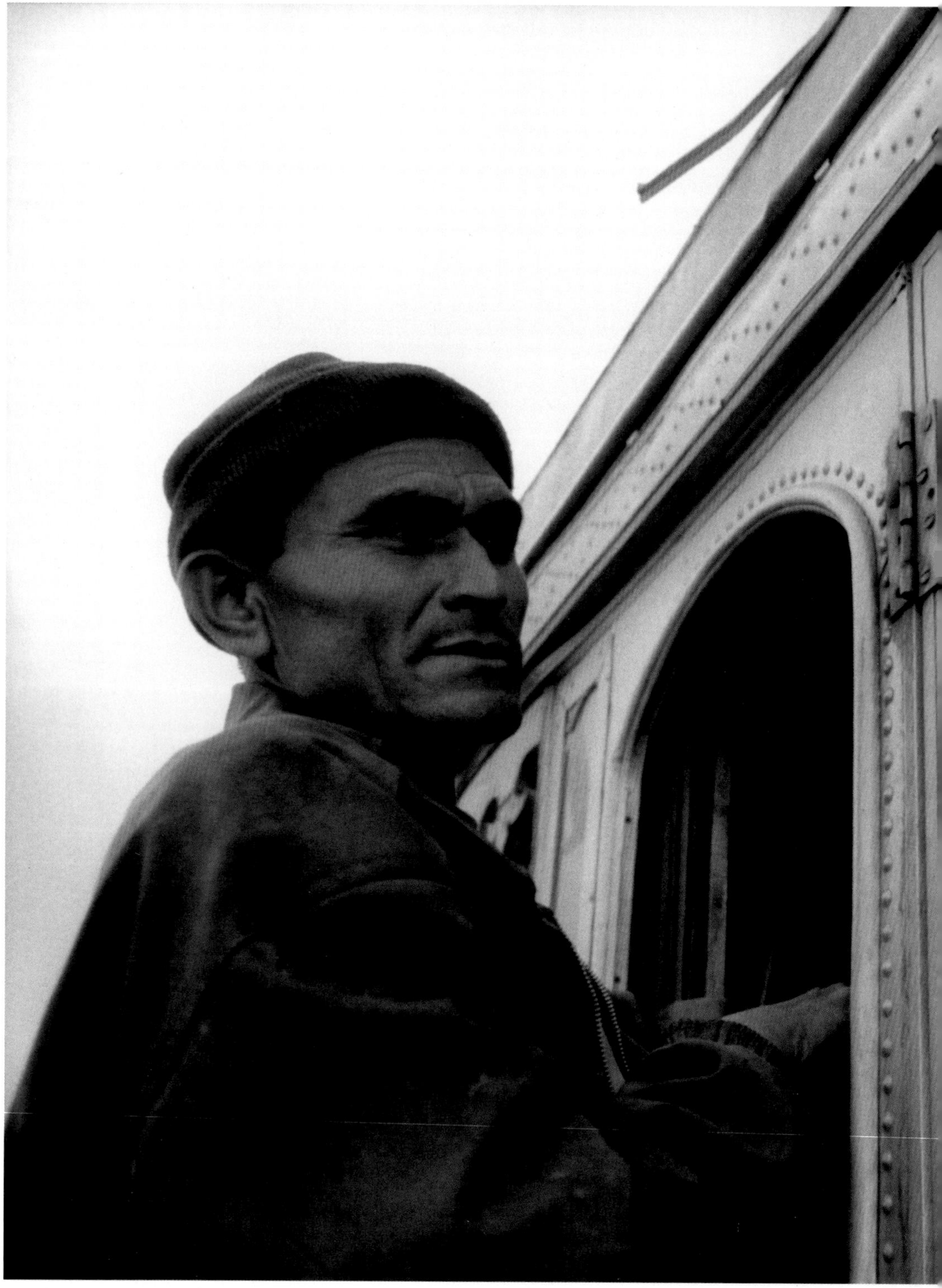

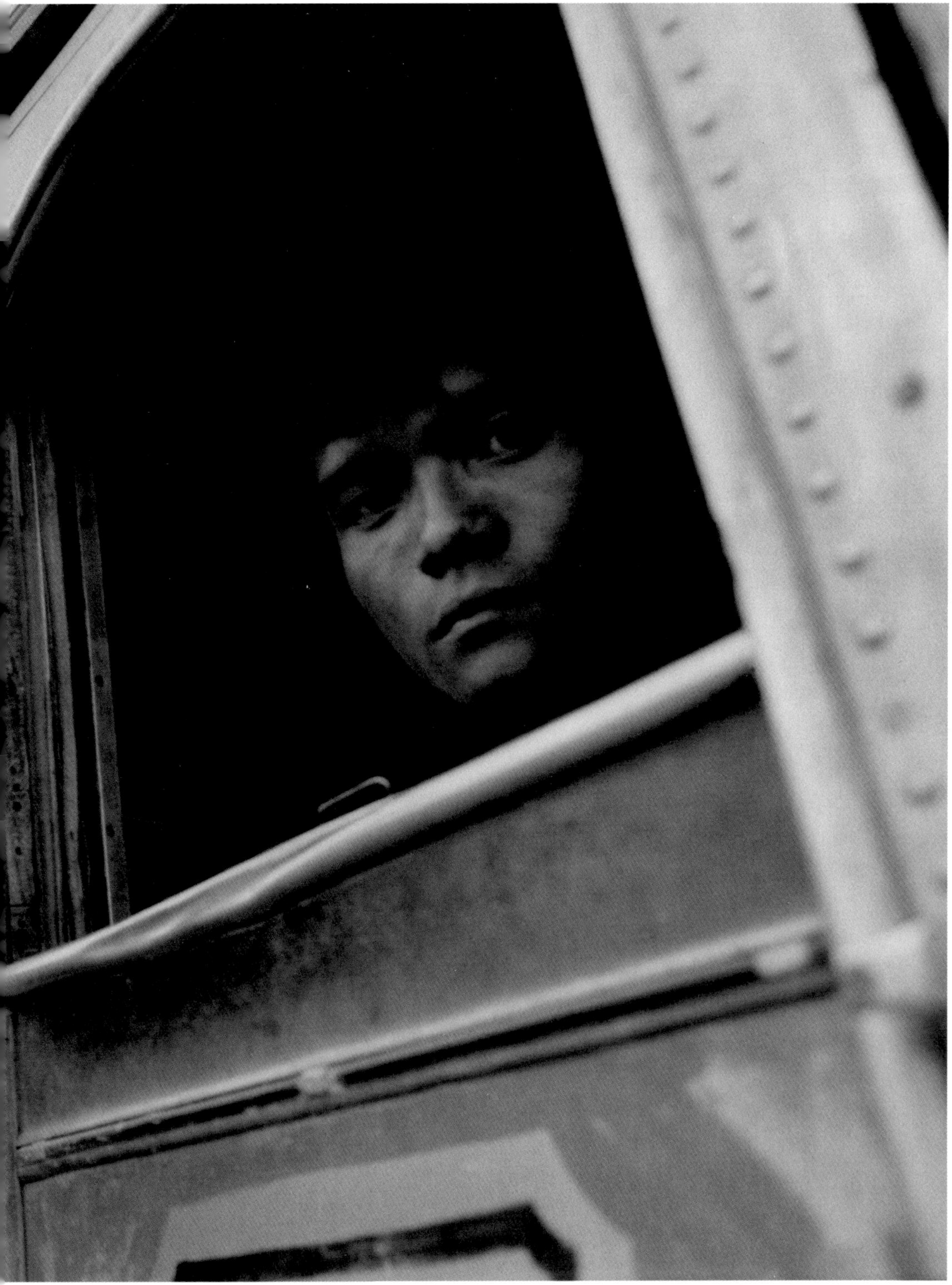

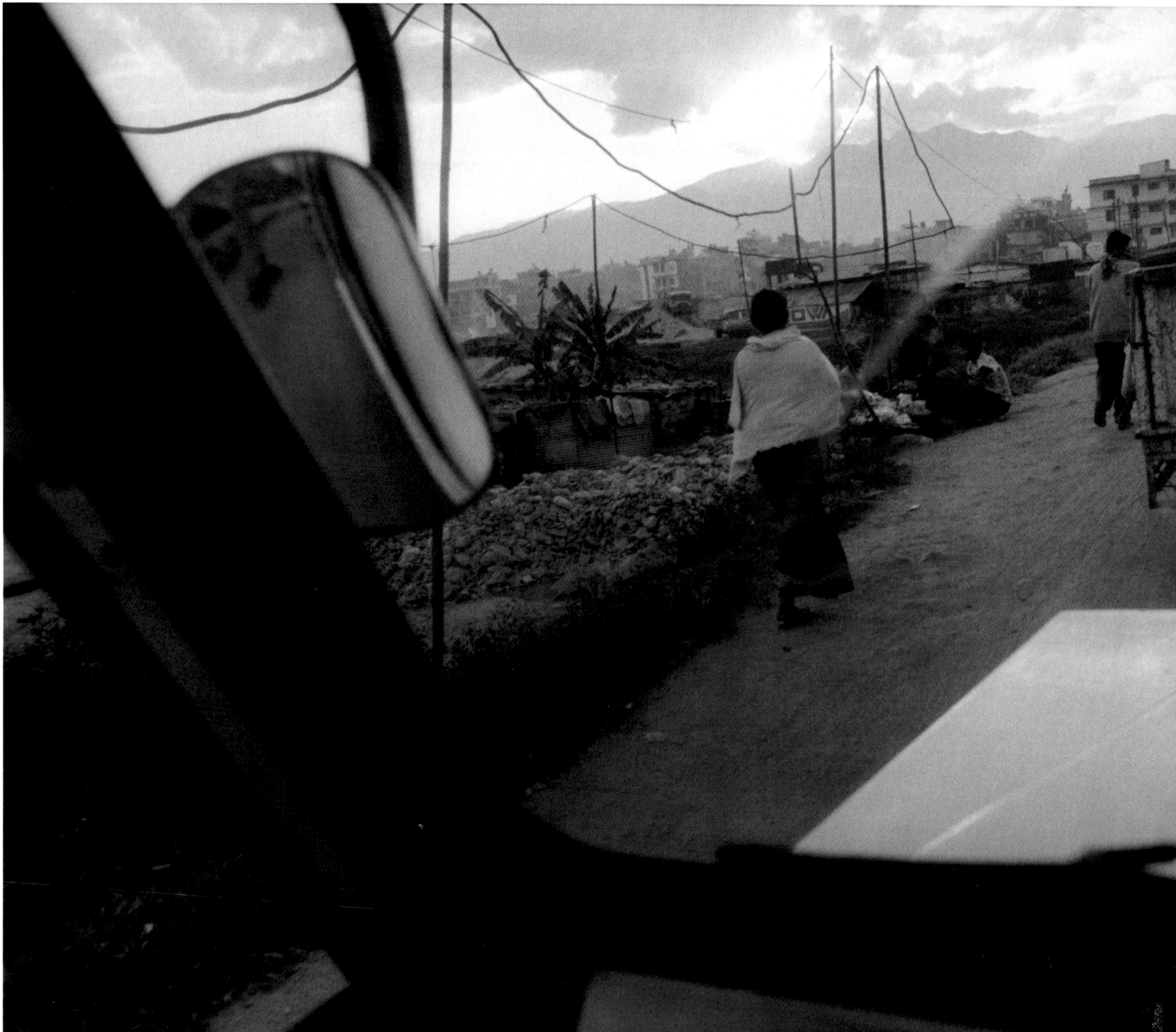

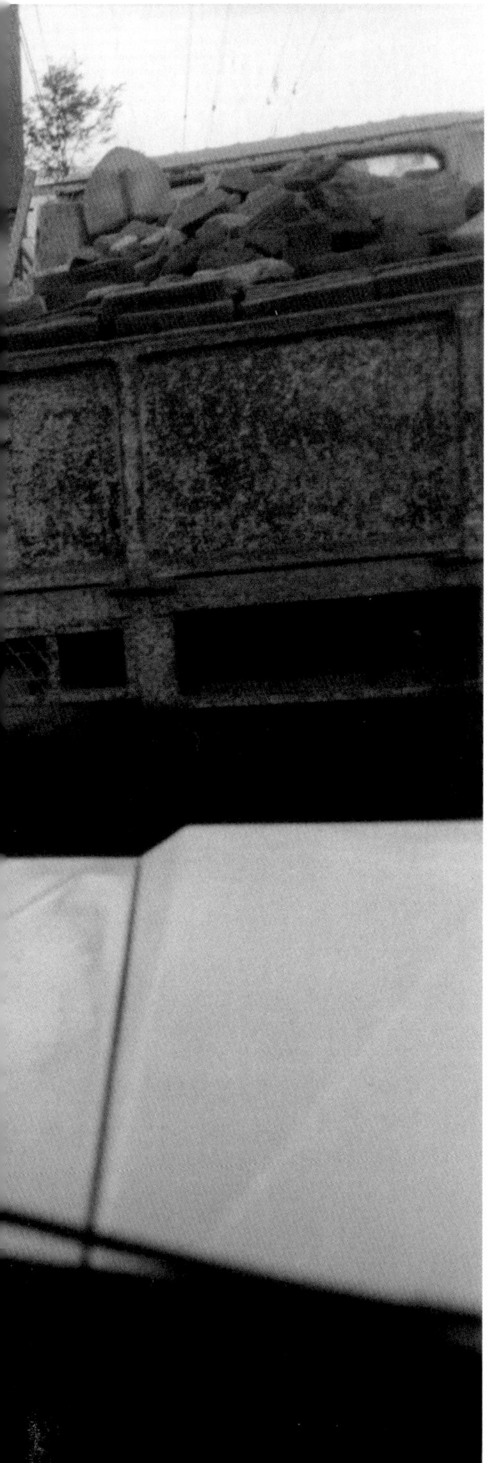

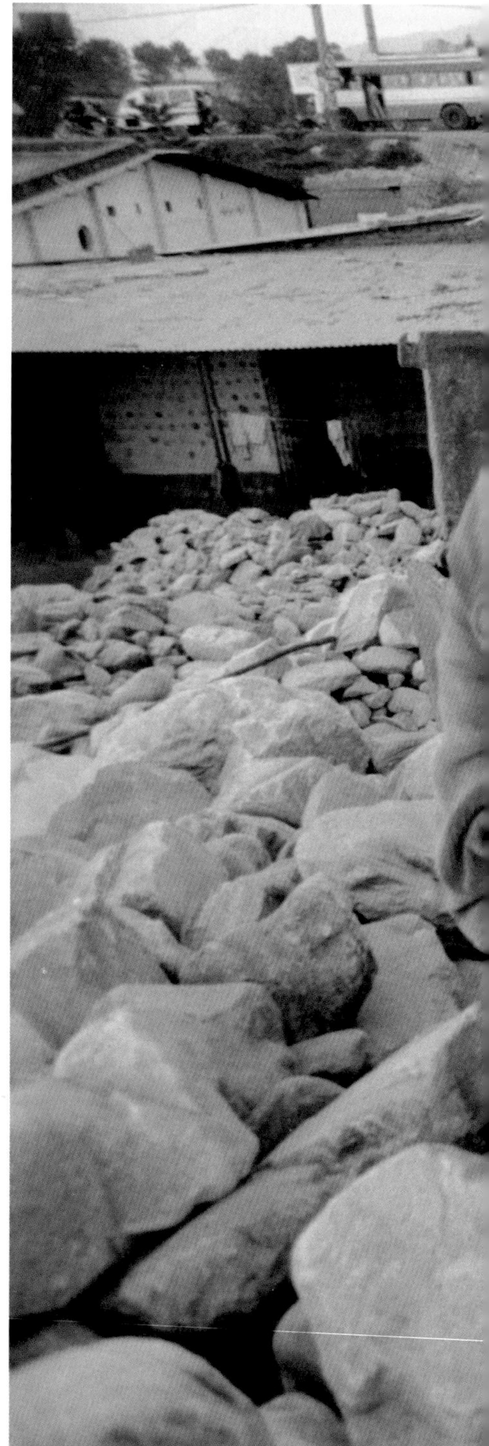

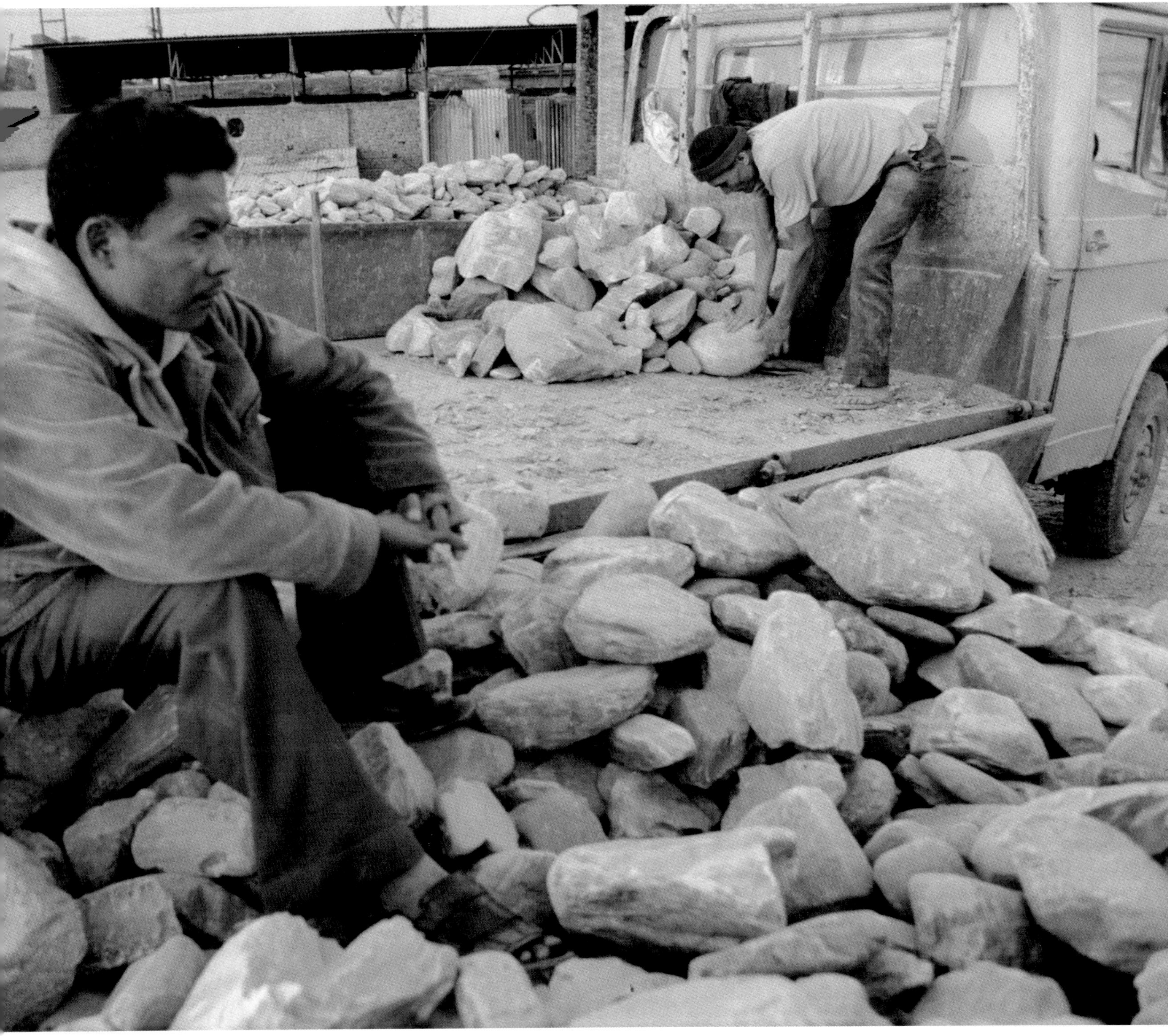

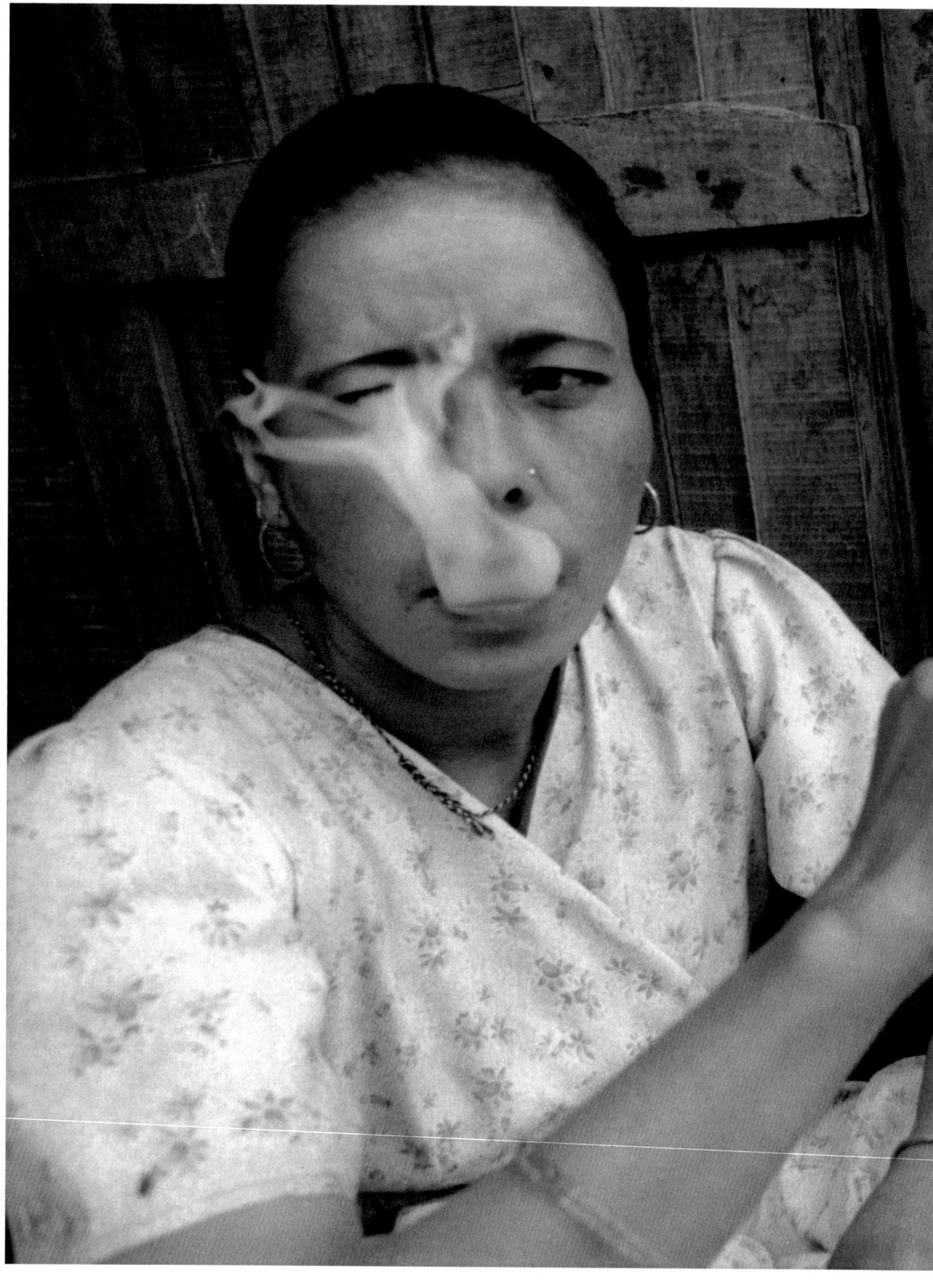

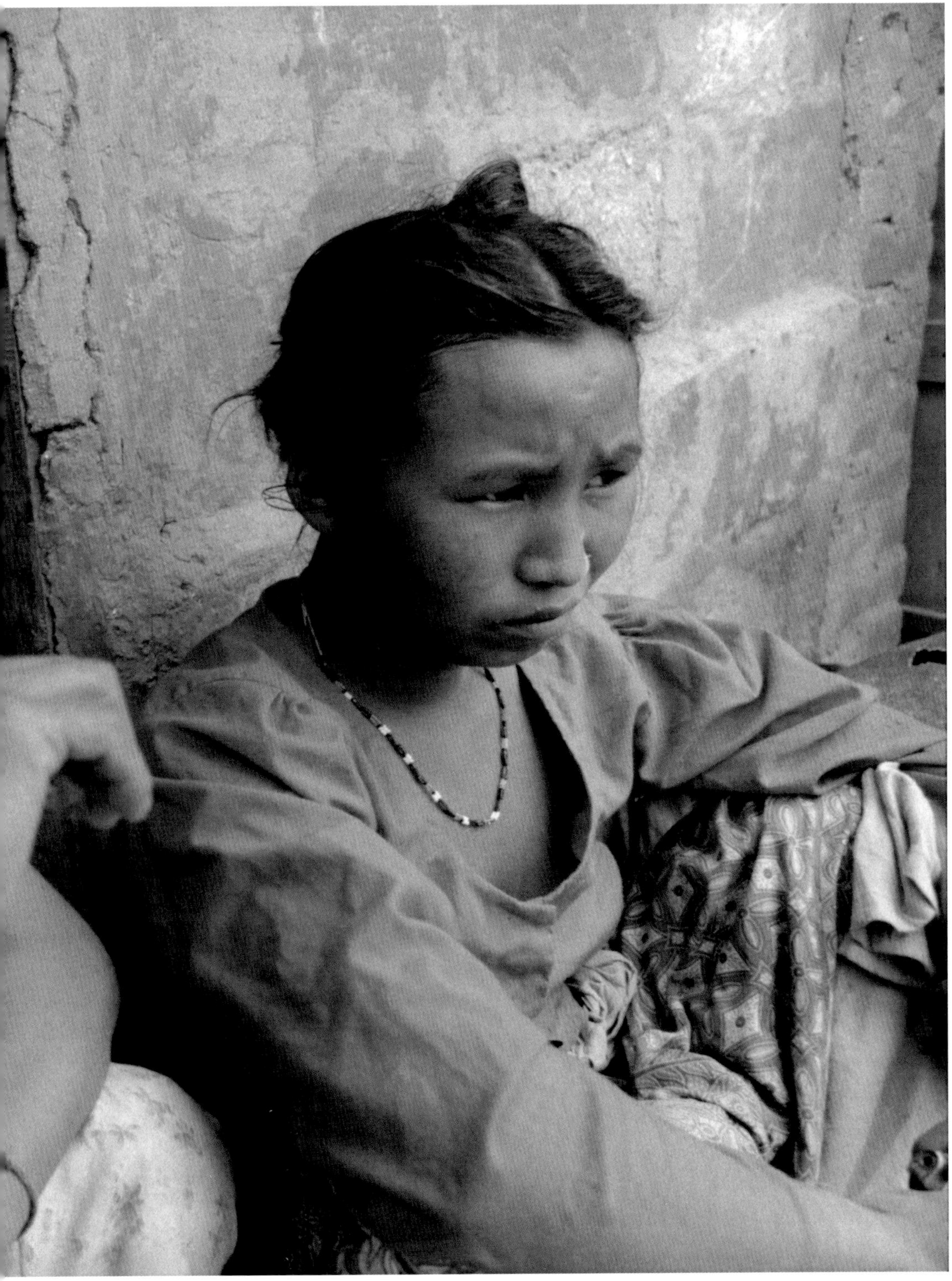

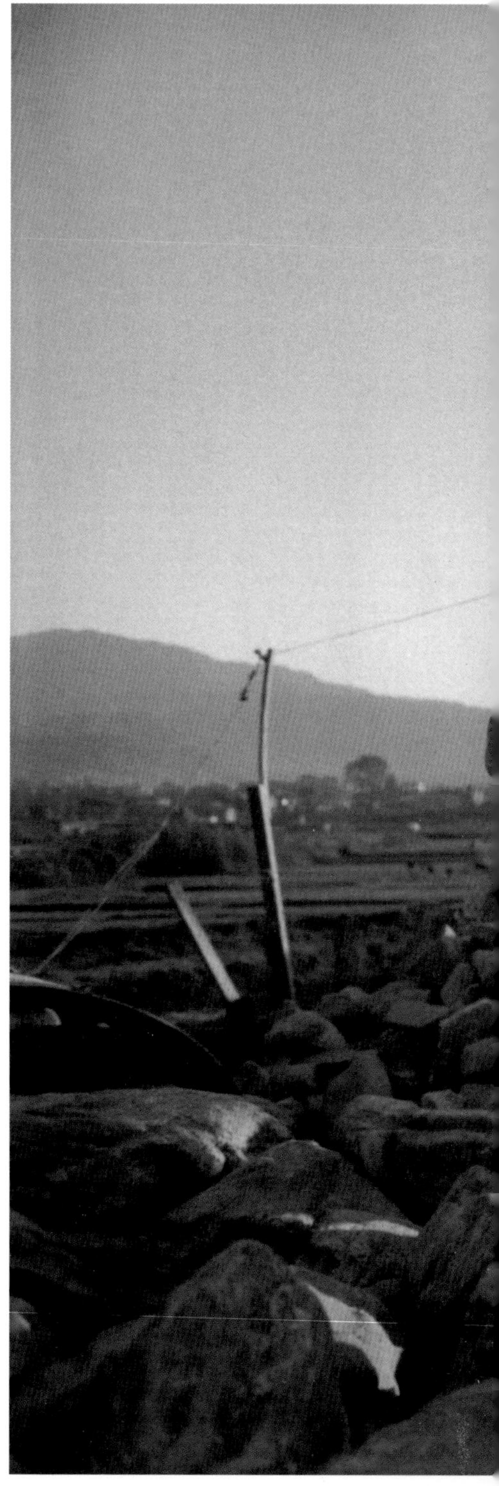

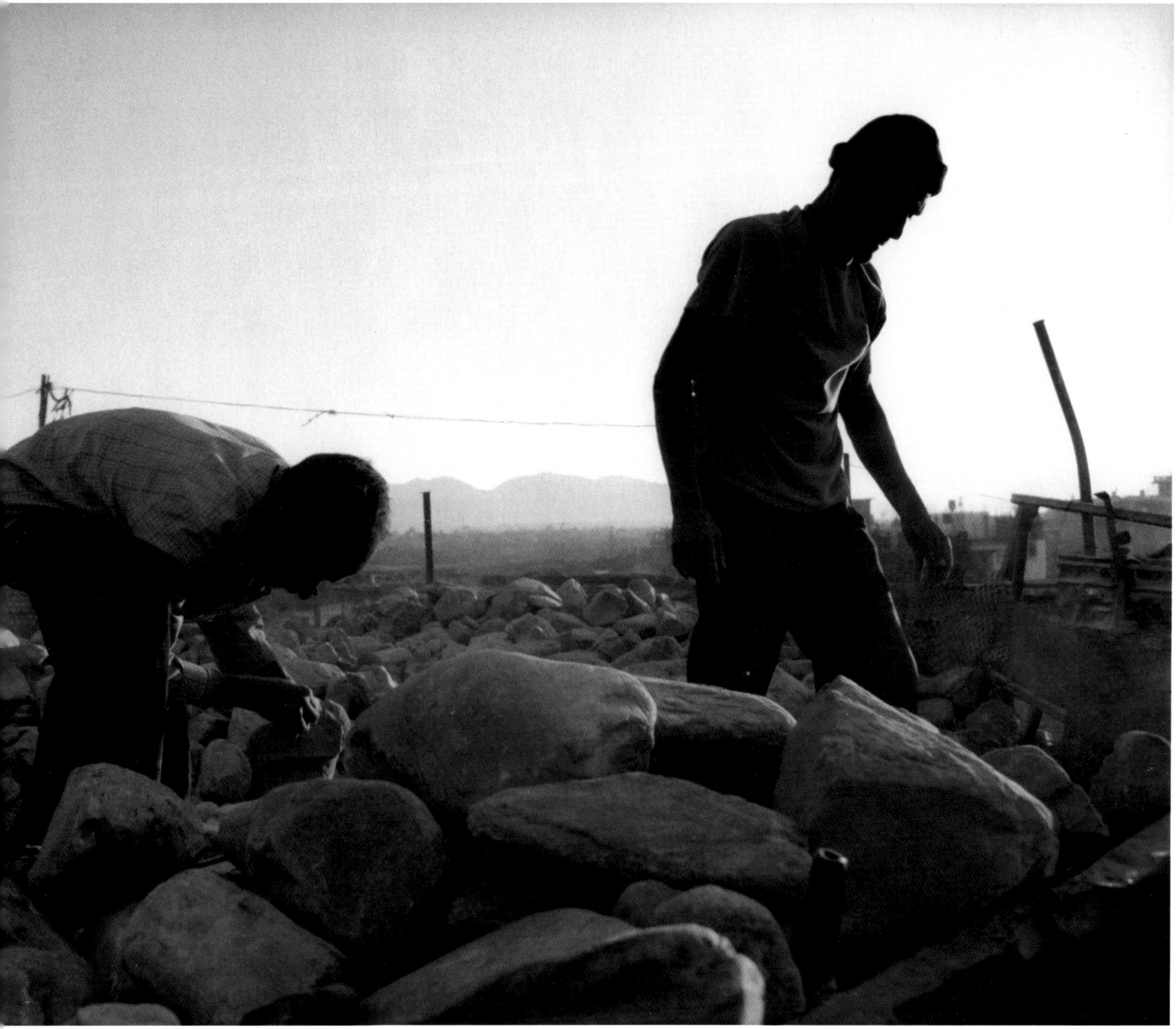

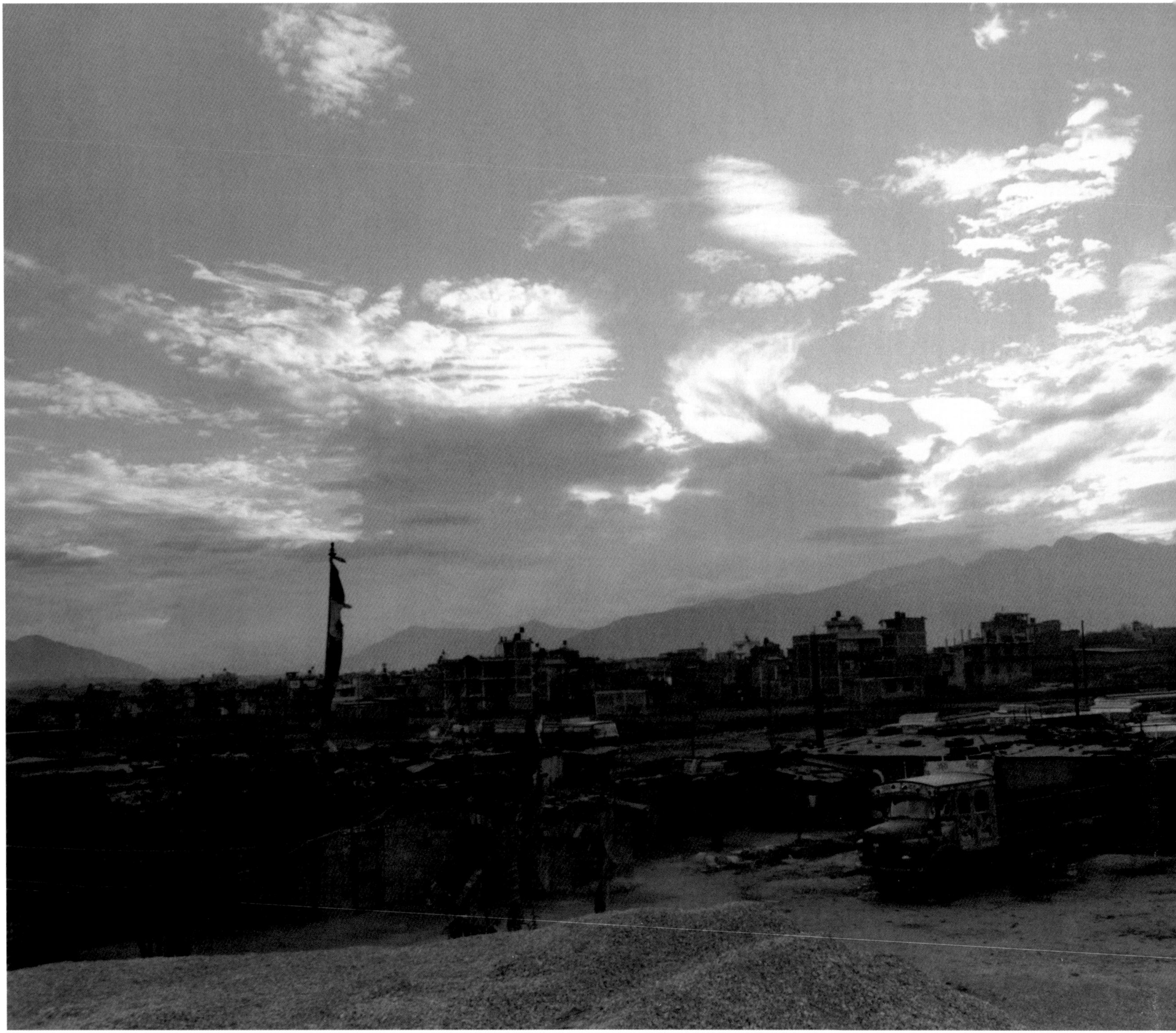

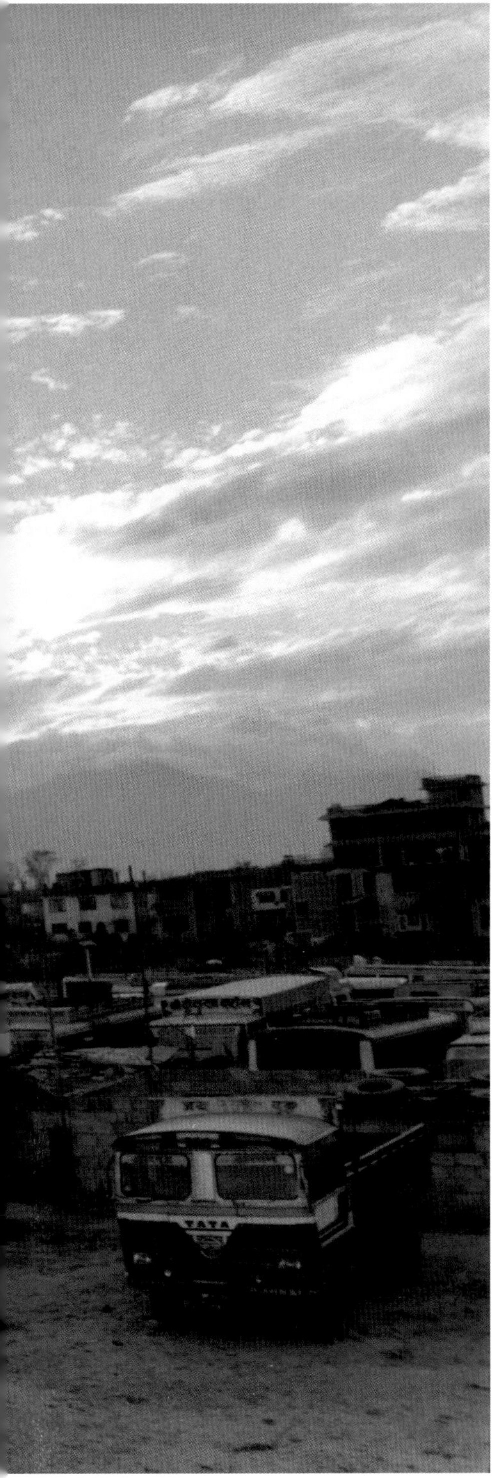
TATA

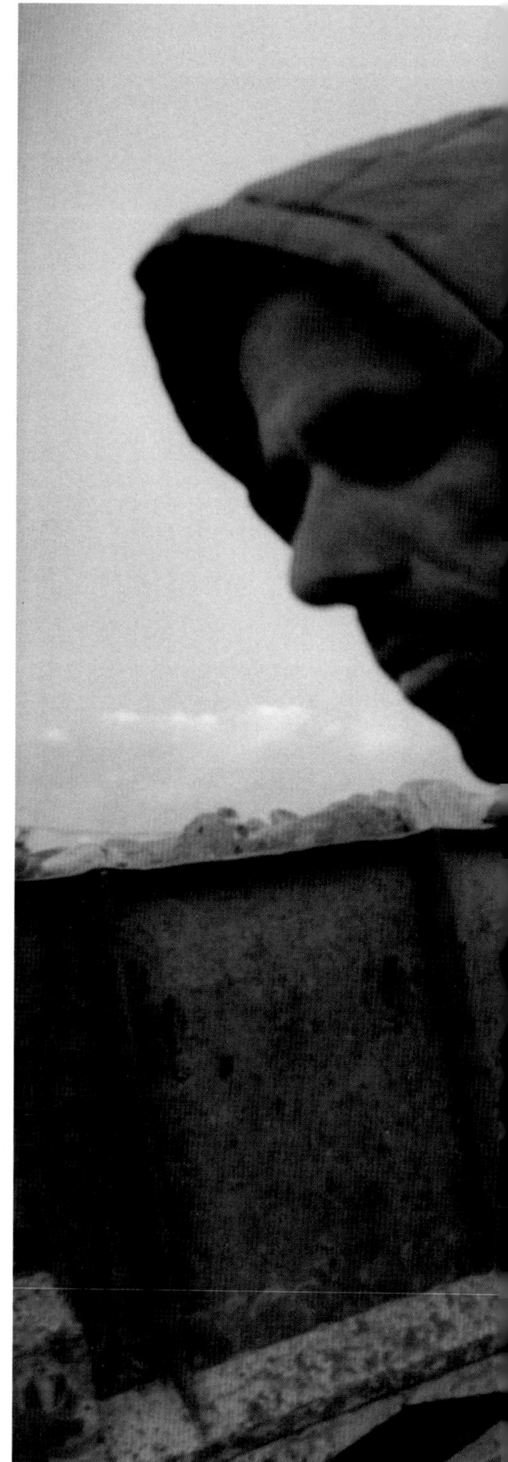

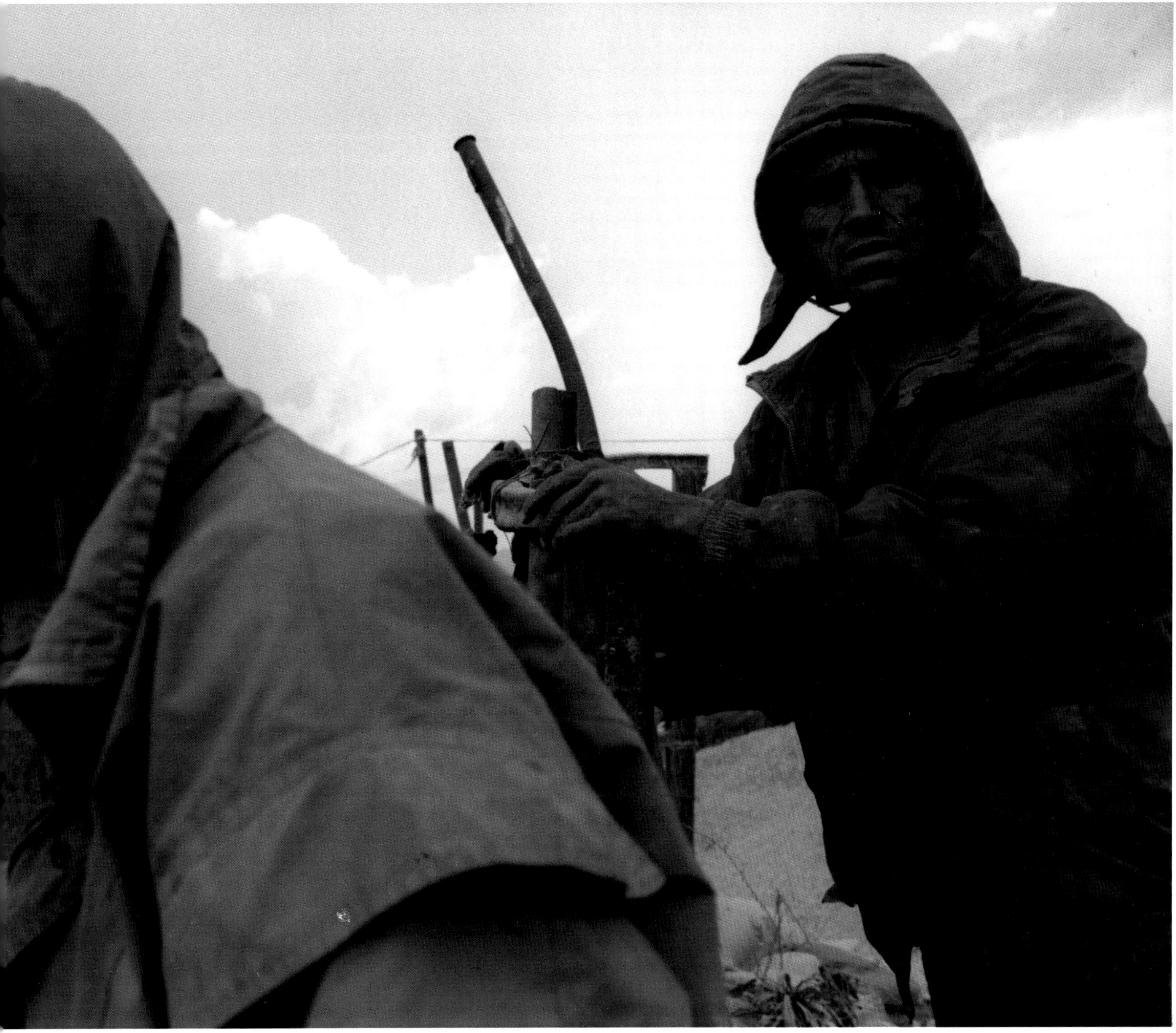

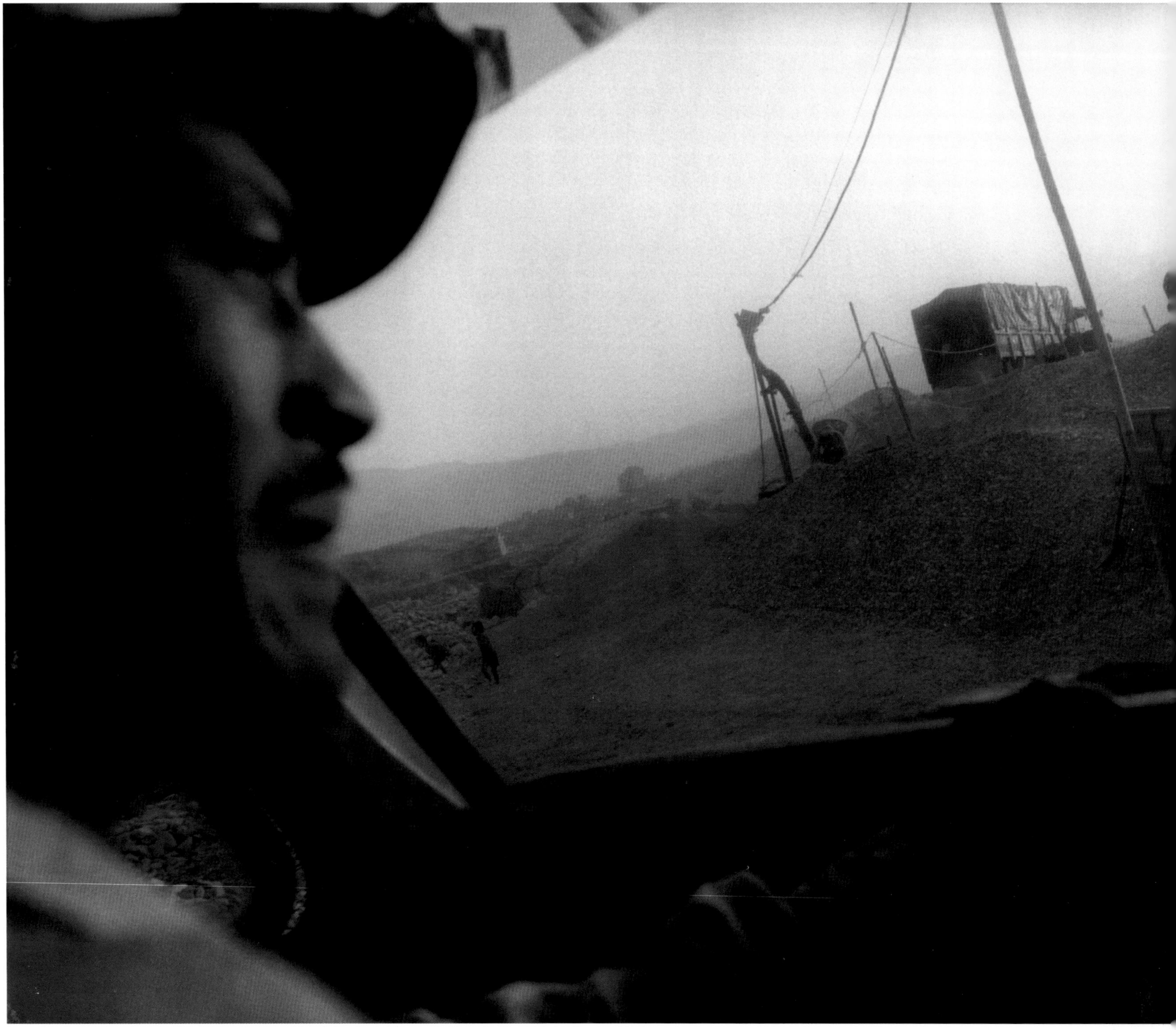

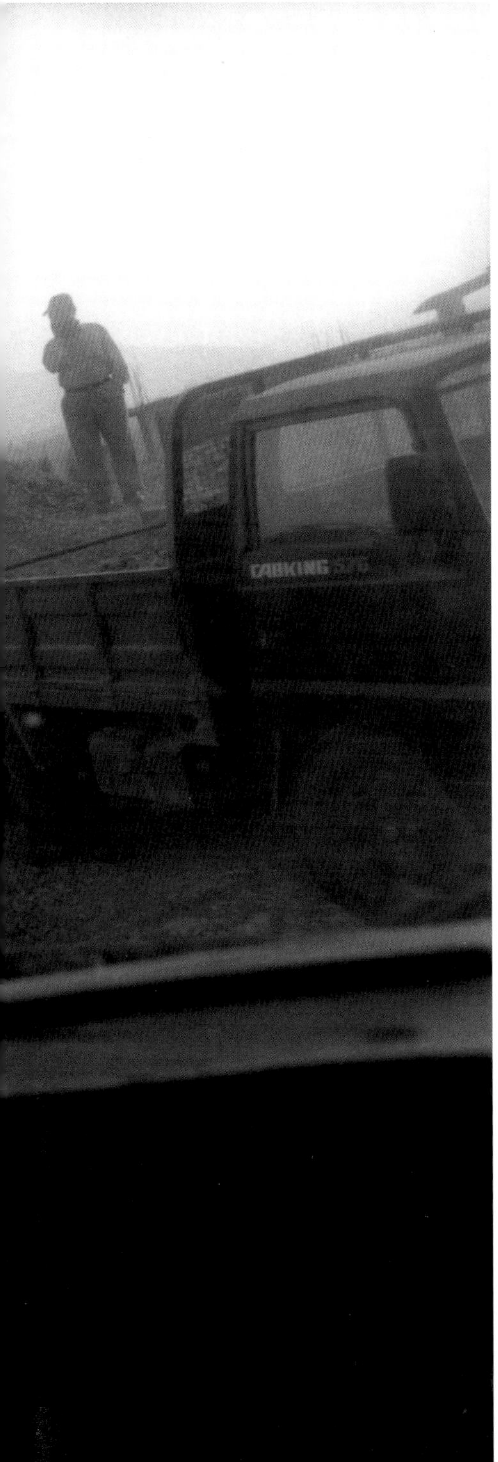
TABKING

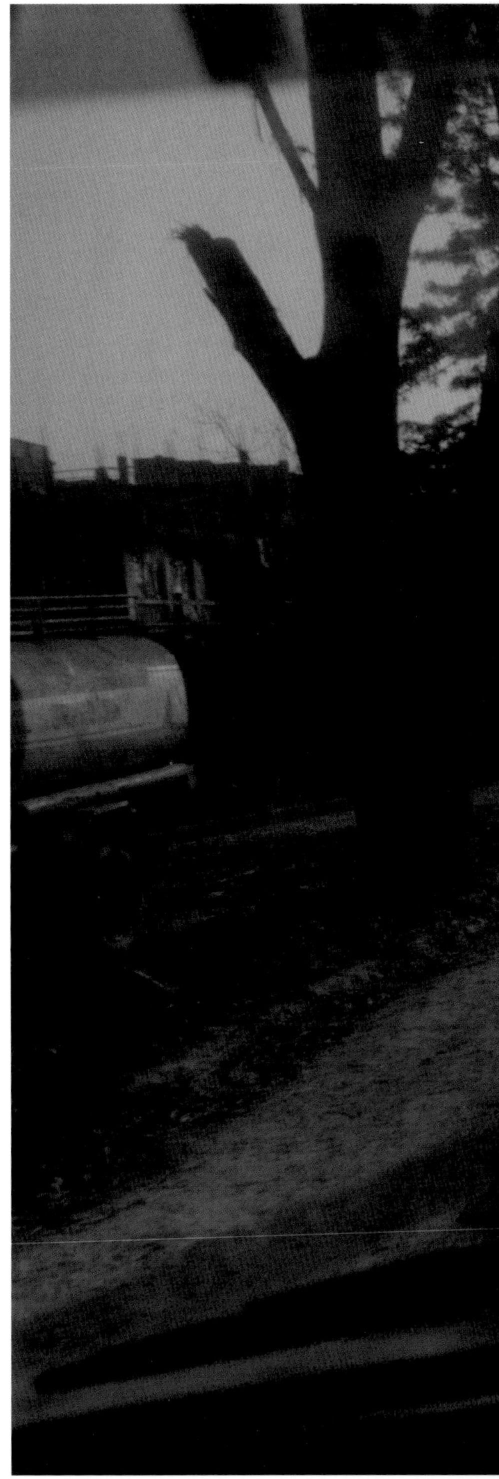

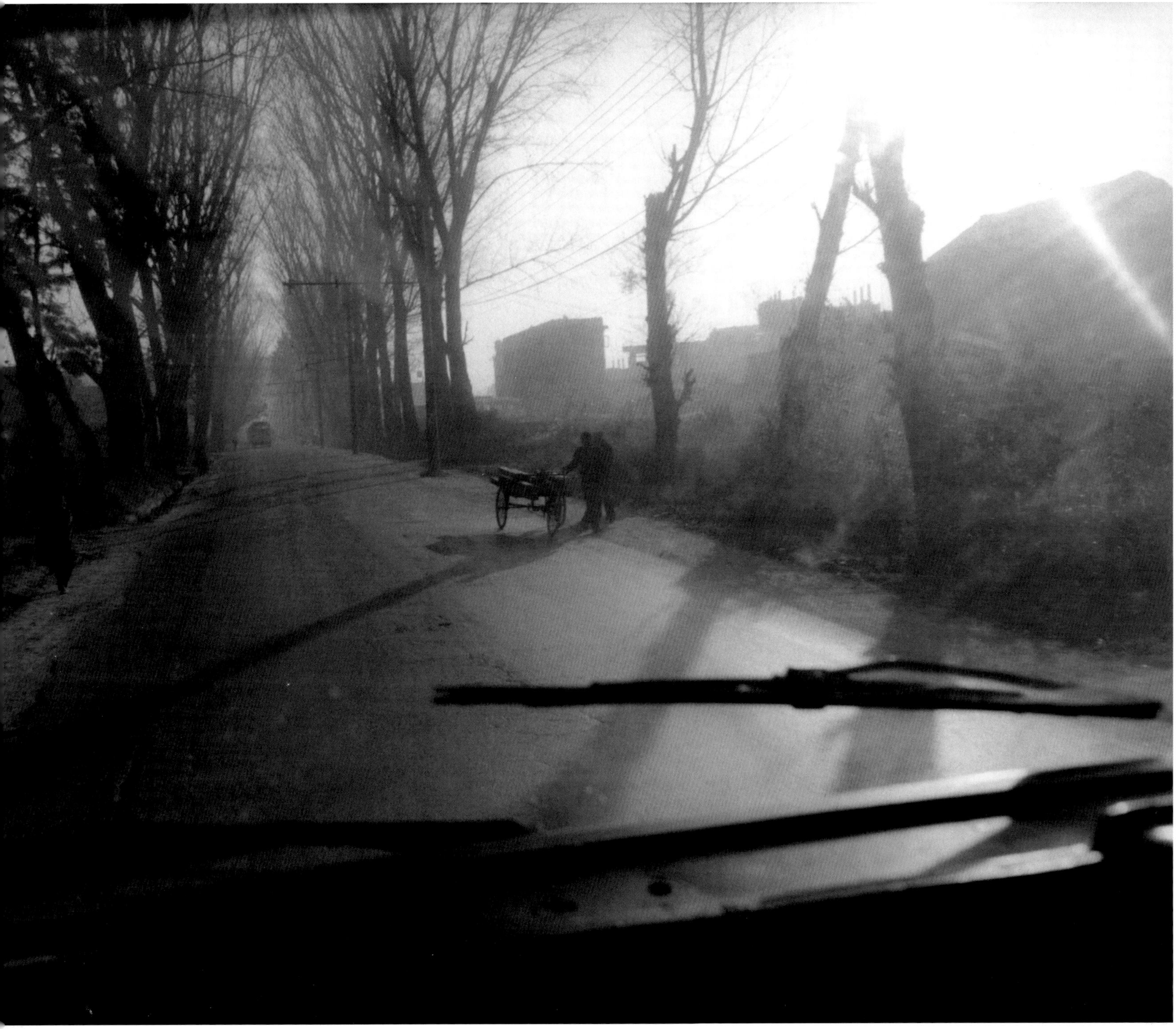

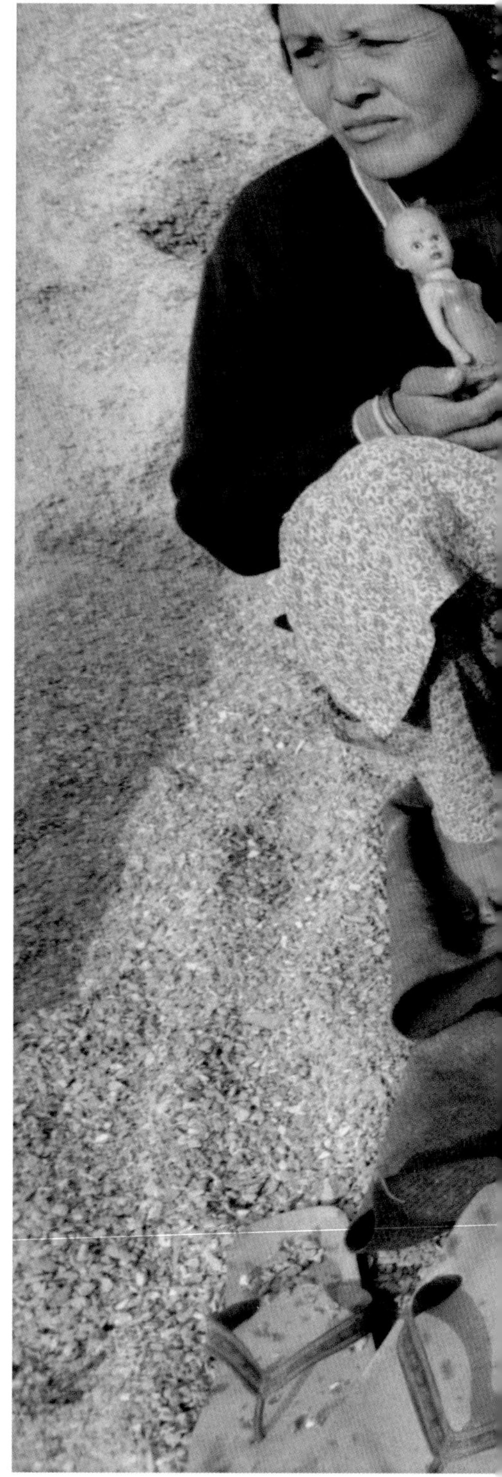

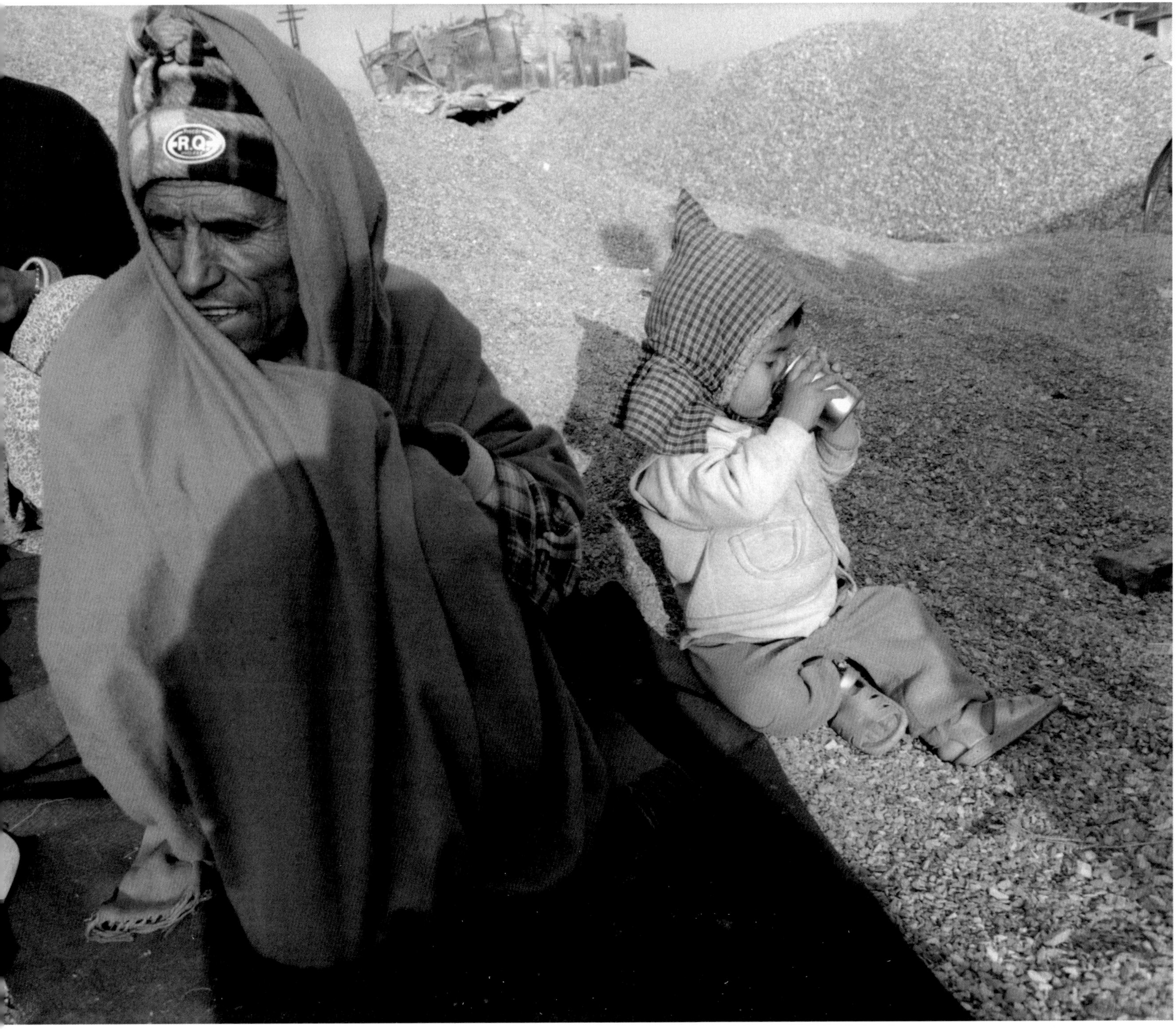
R.Q

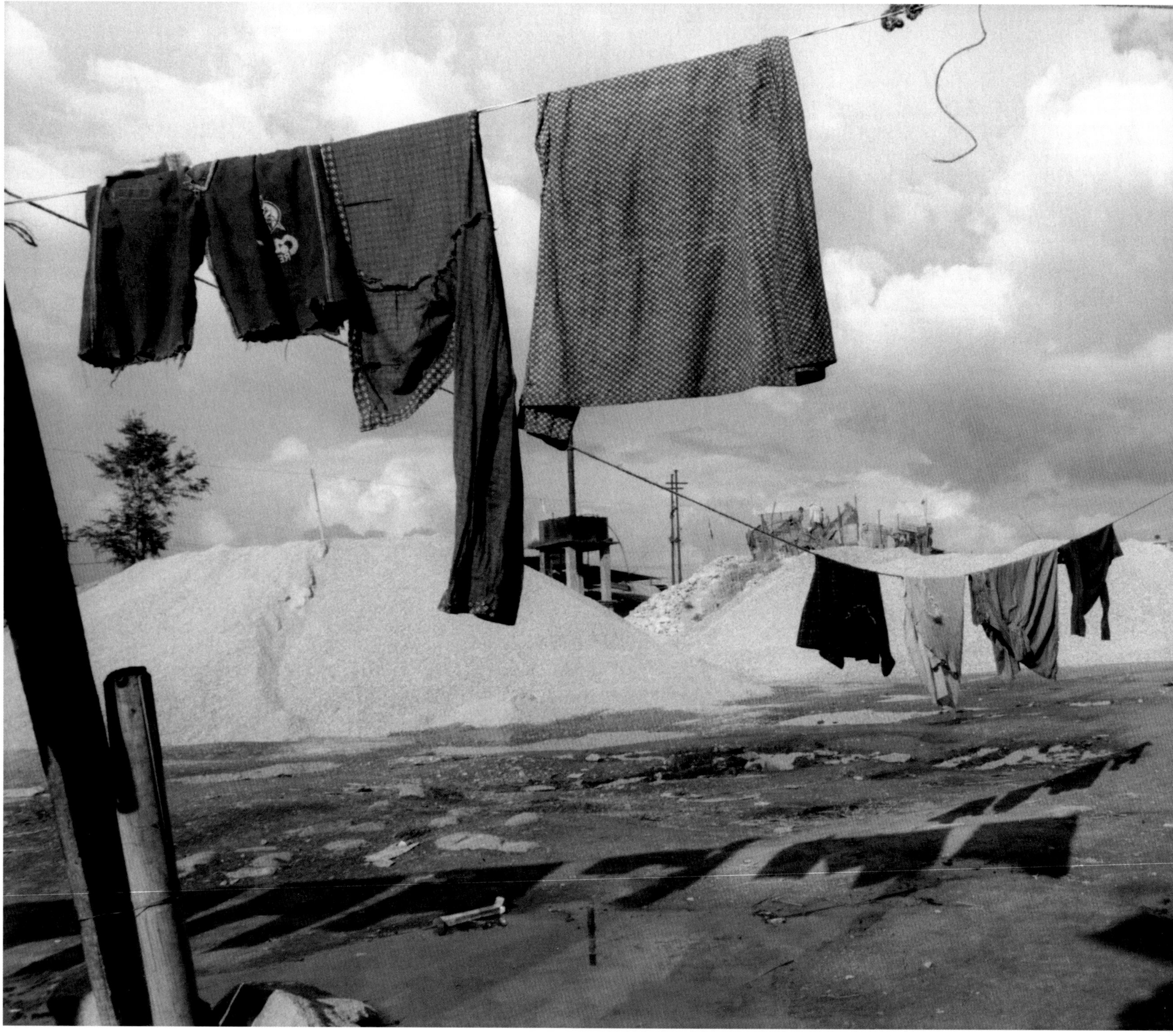

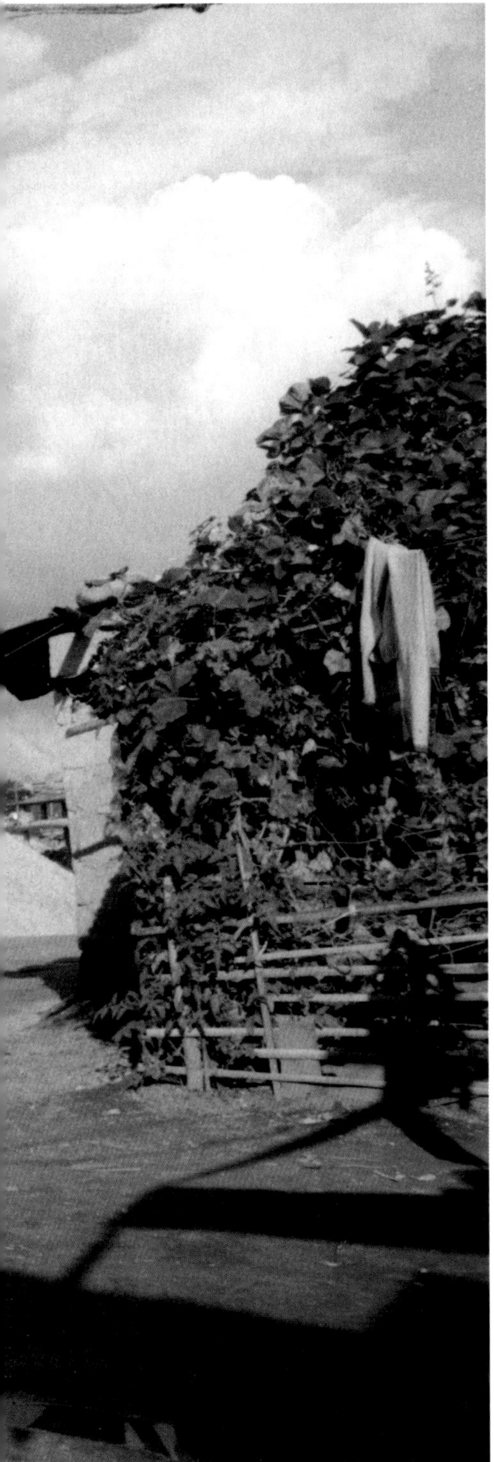

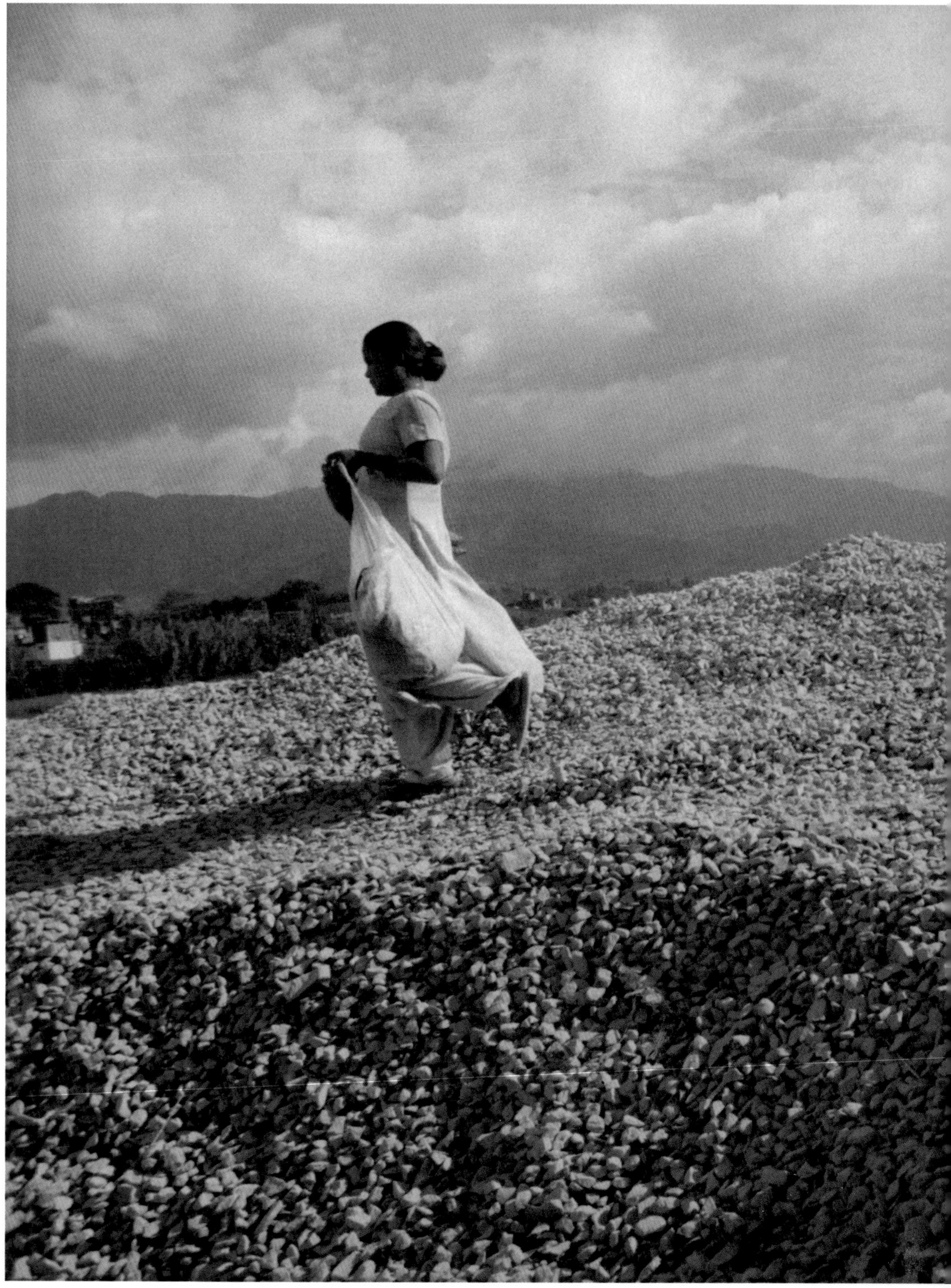

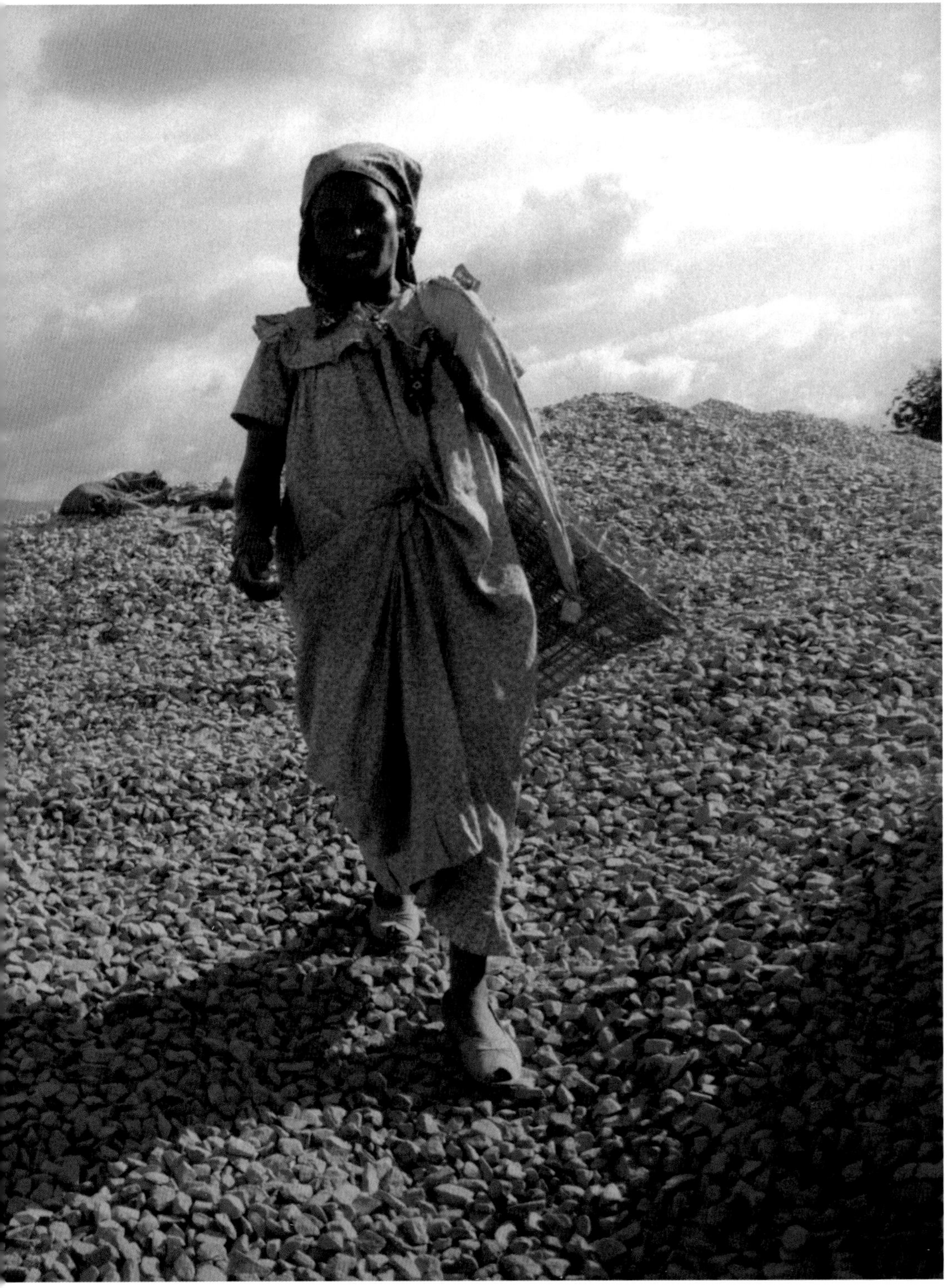

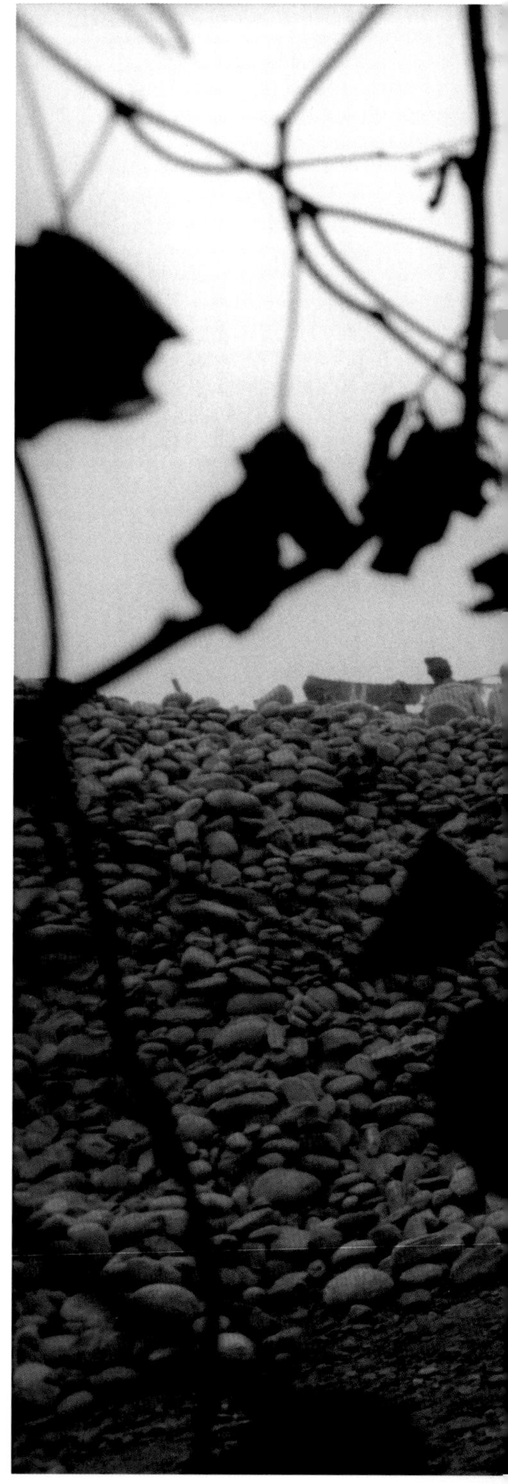

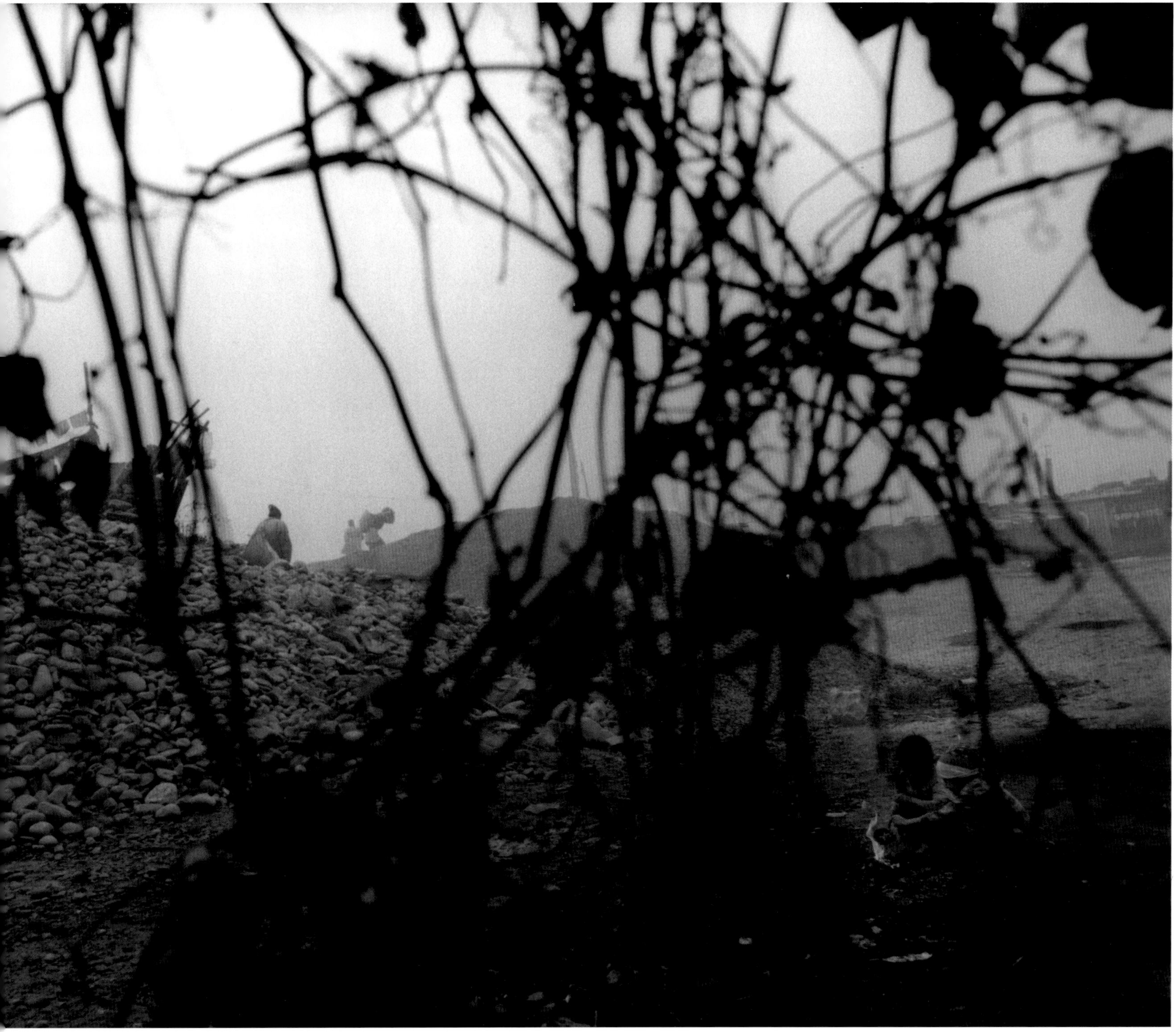

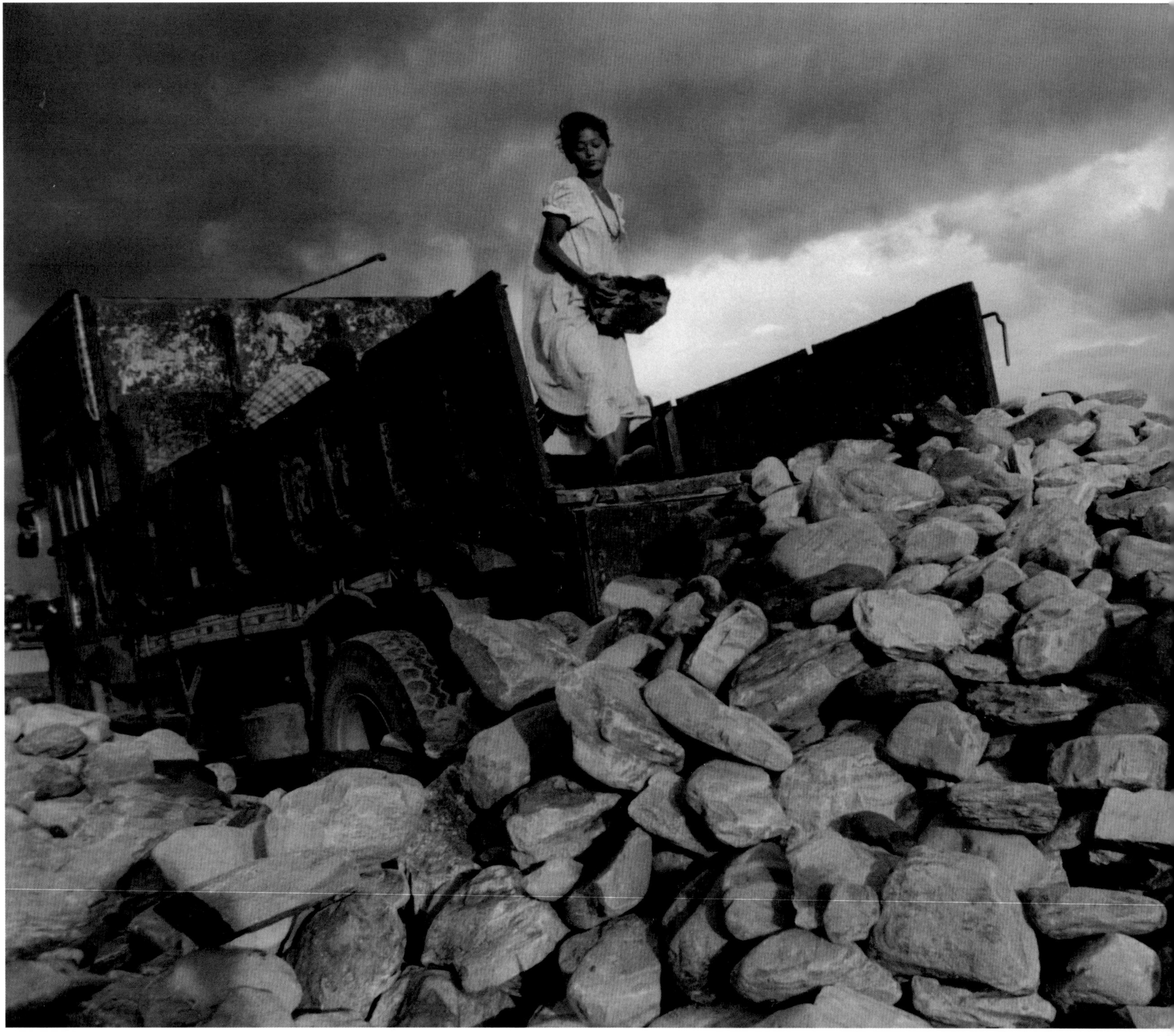

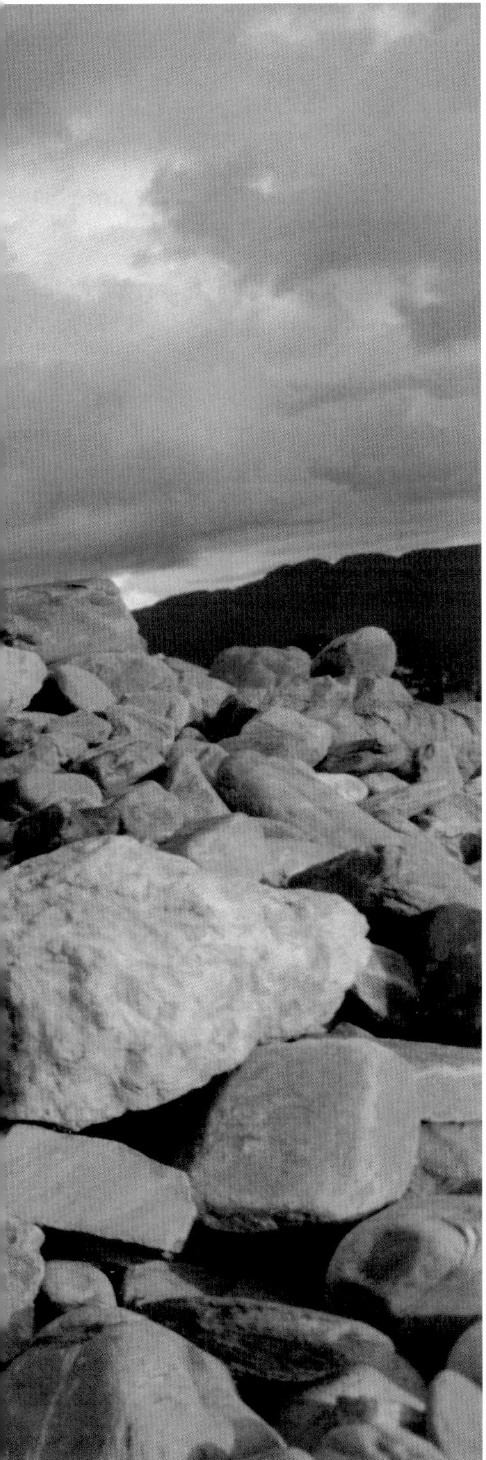

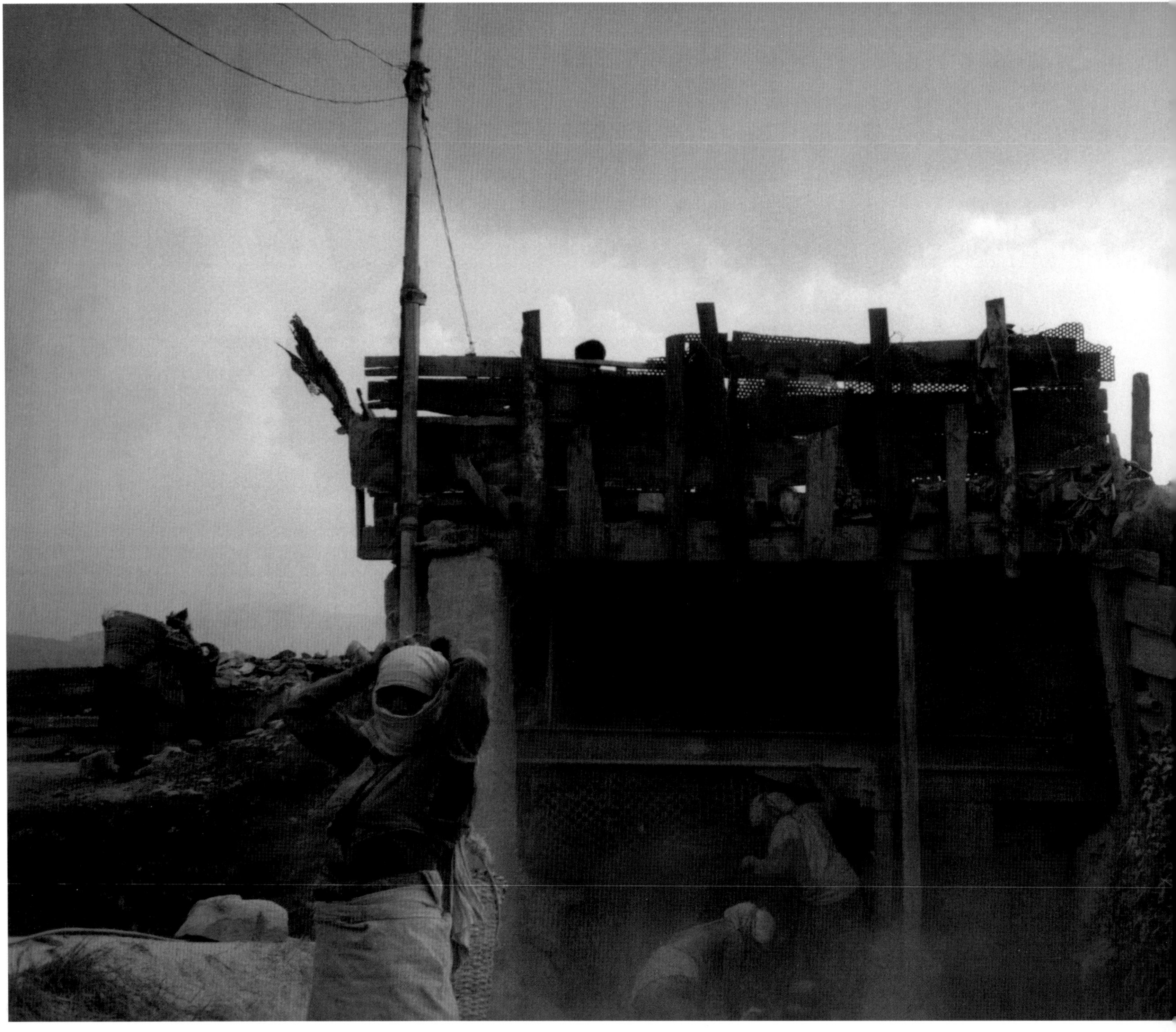

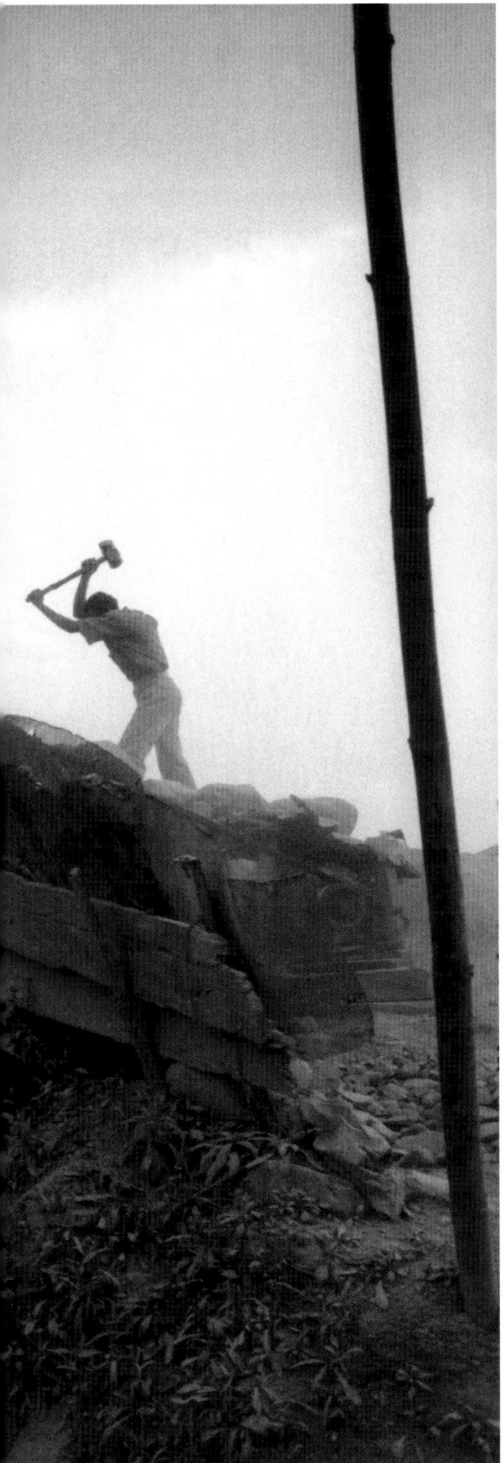

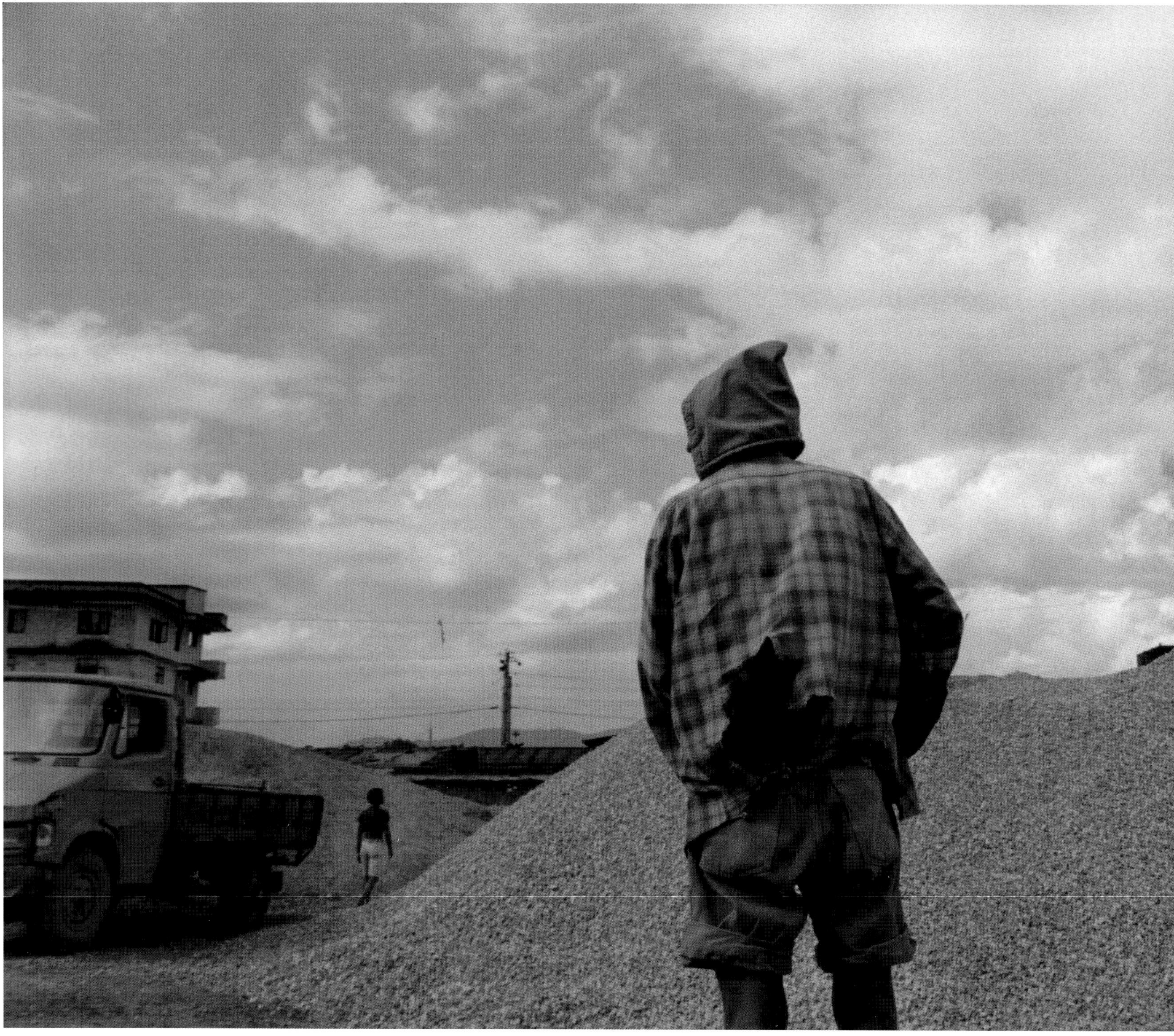

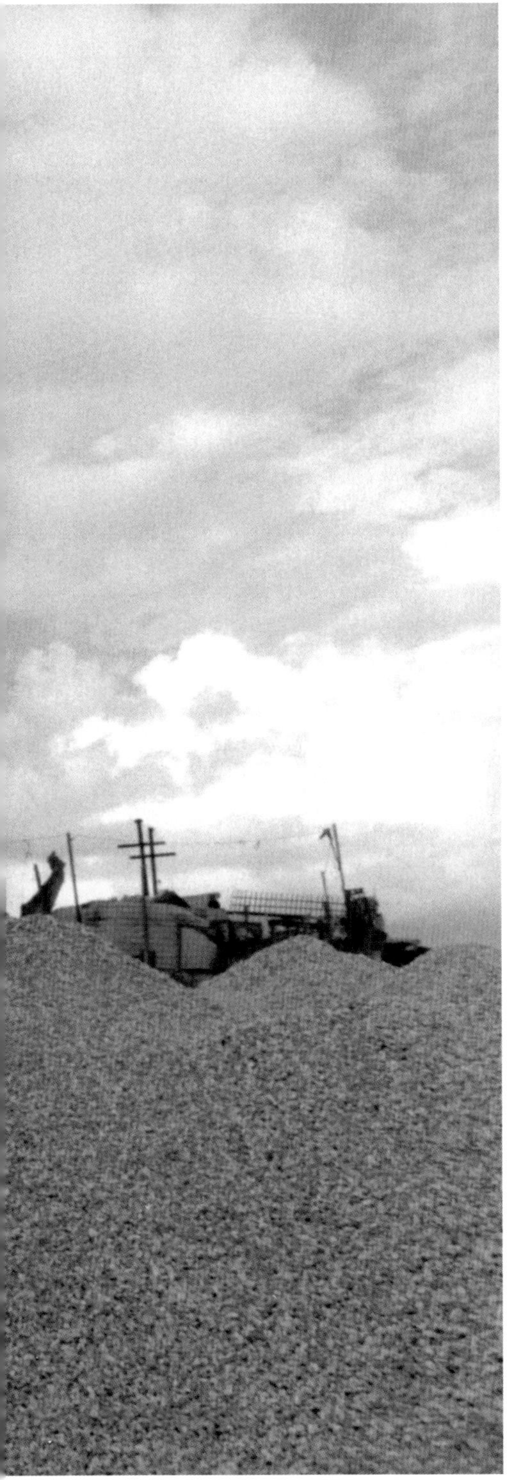

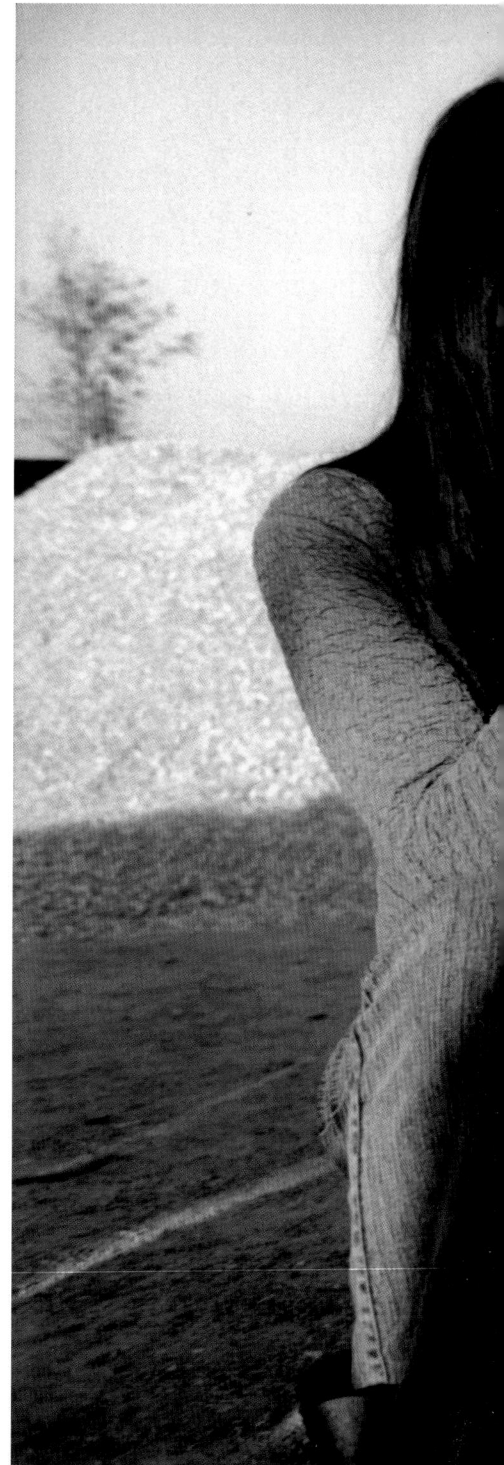

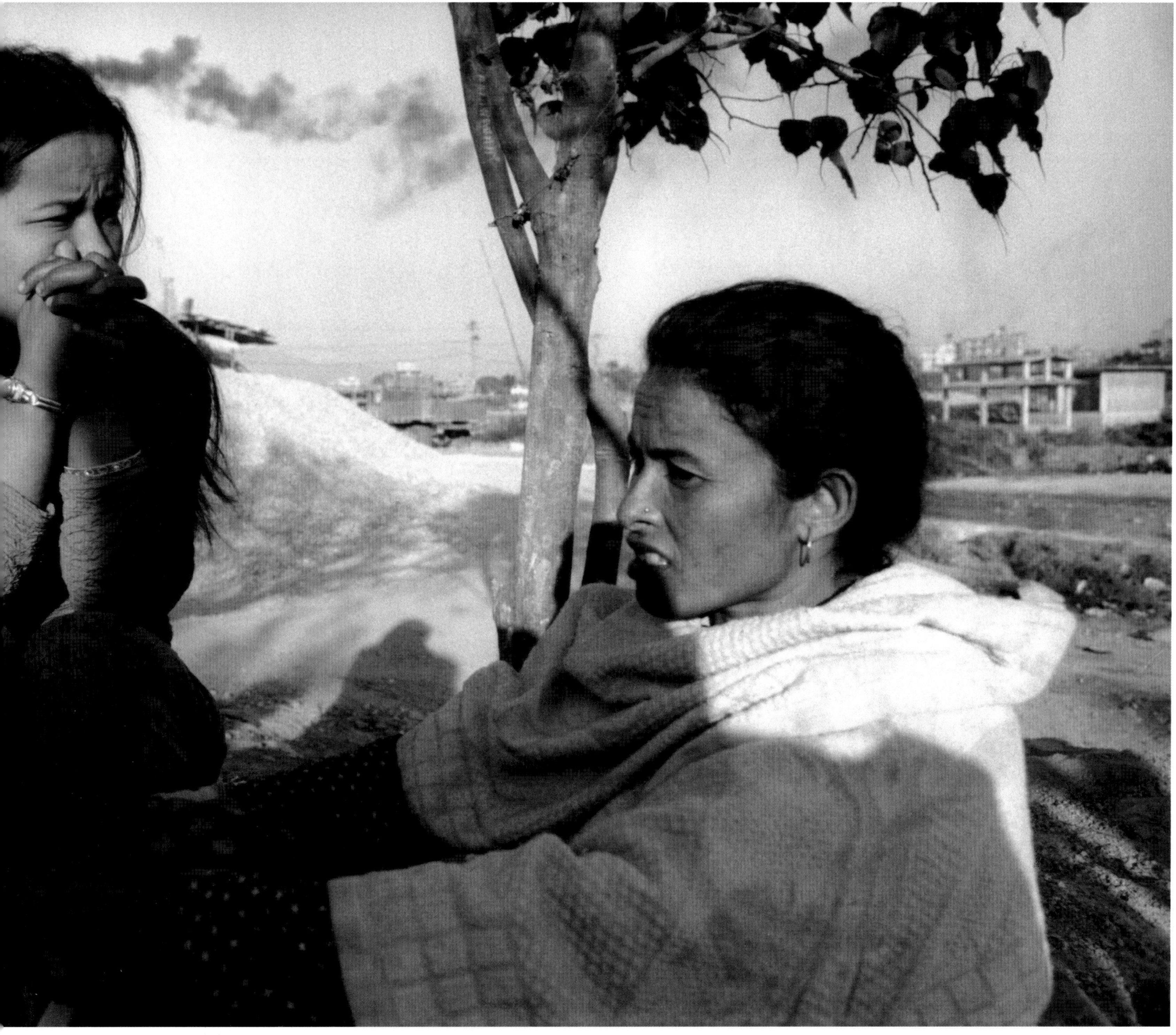

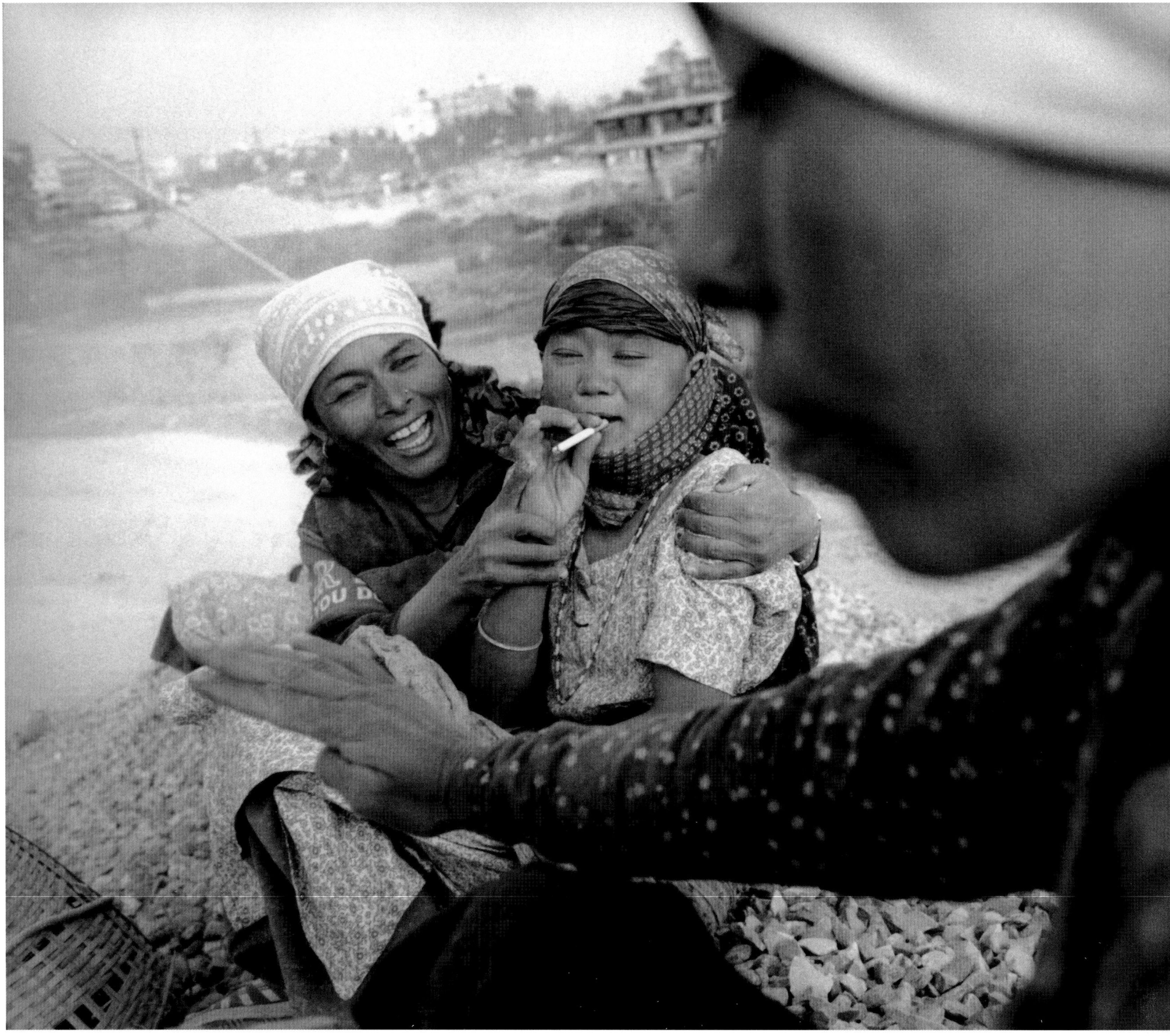

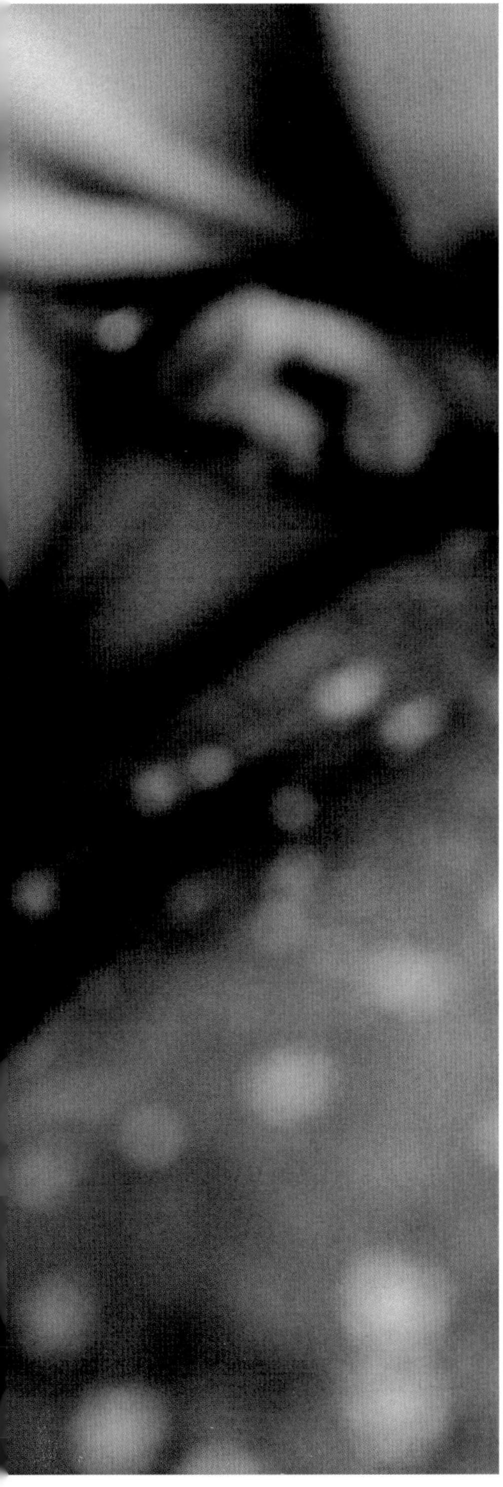

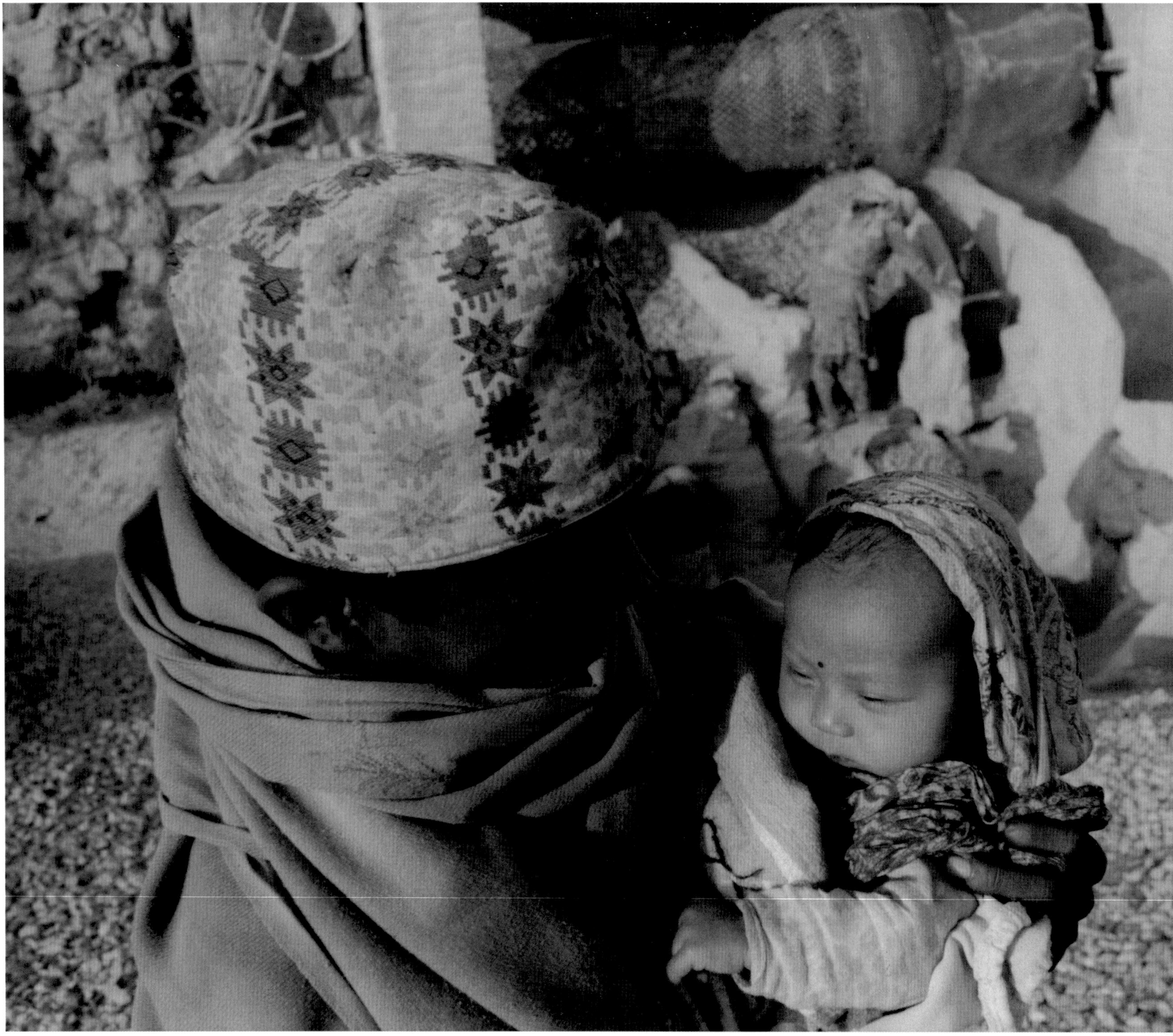

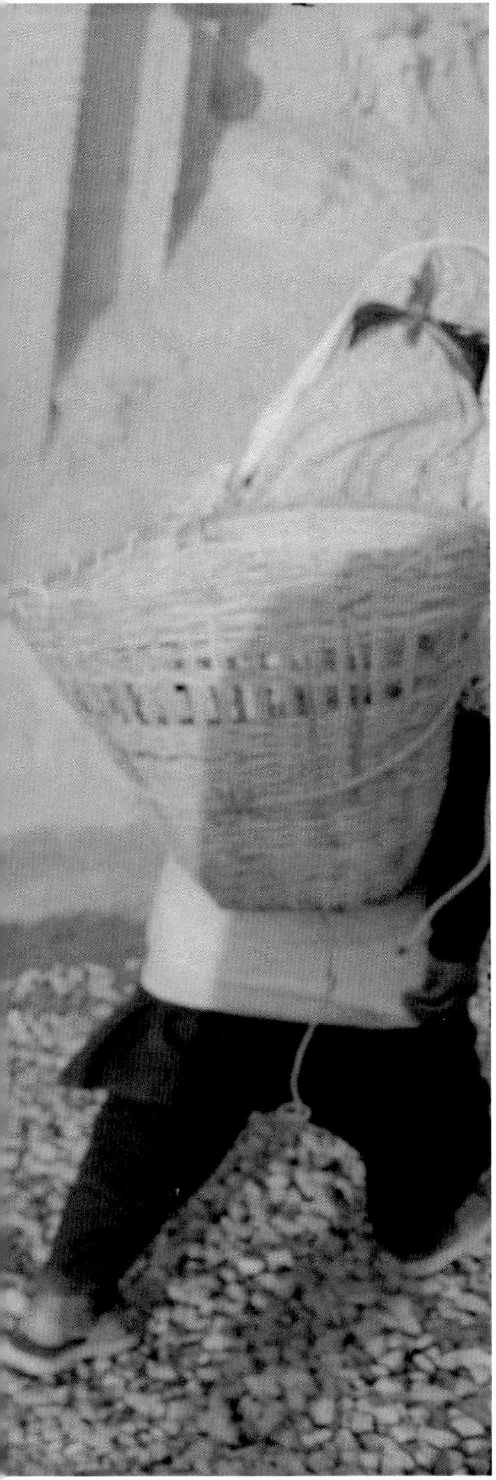

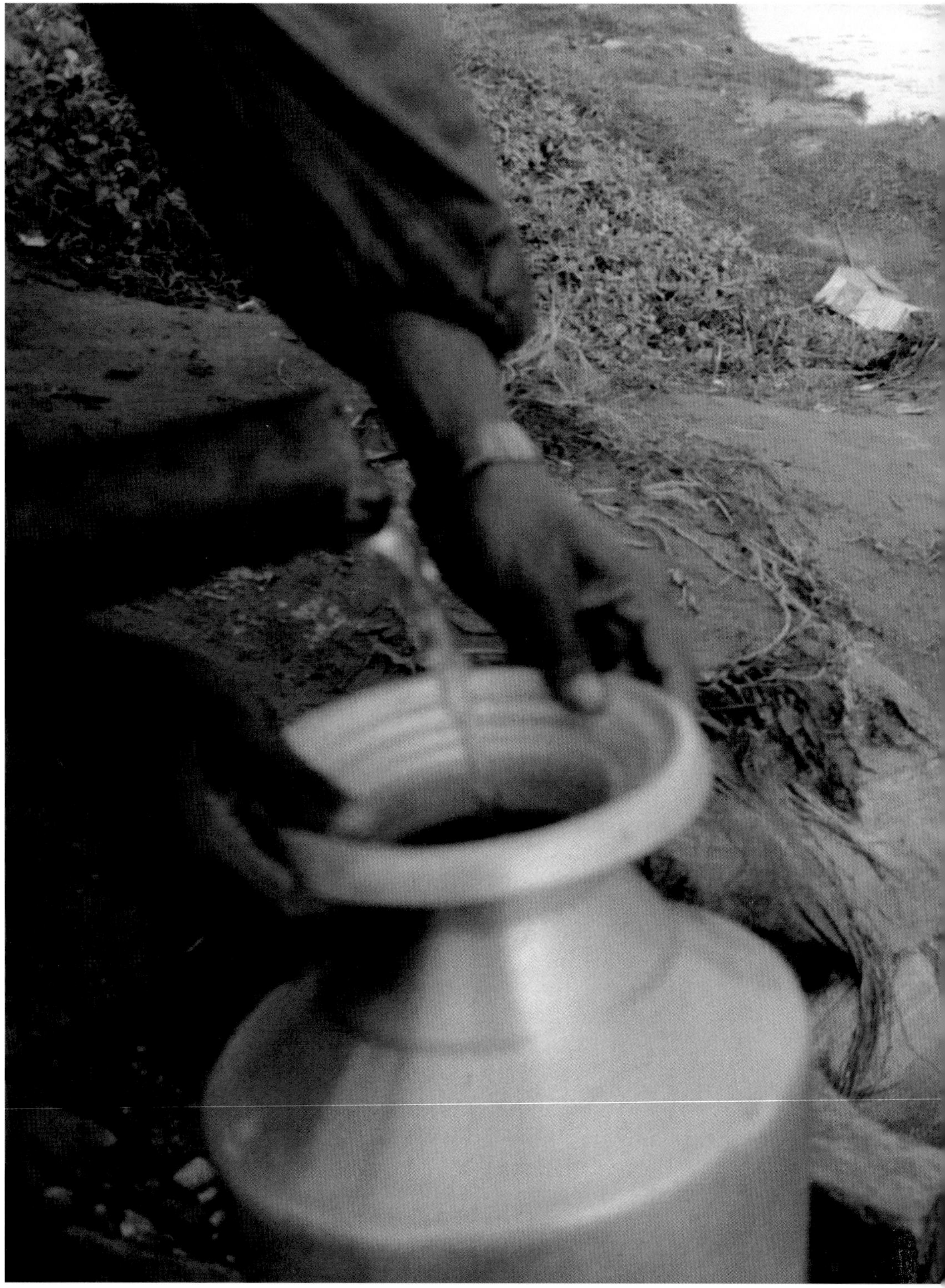

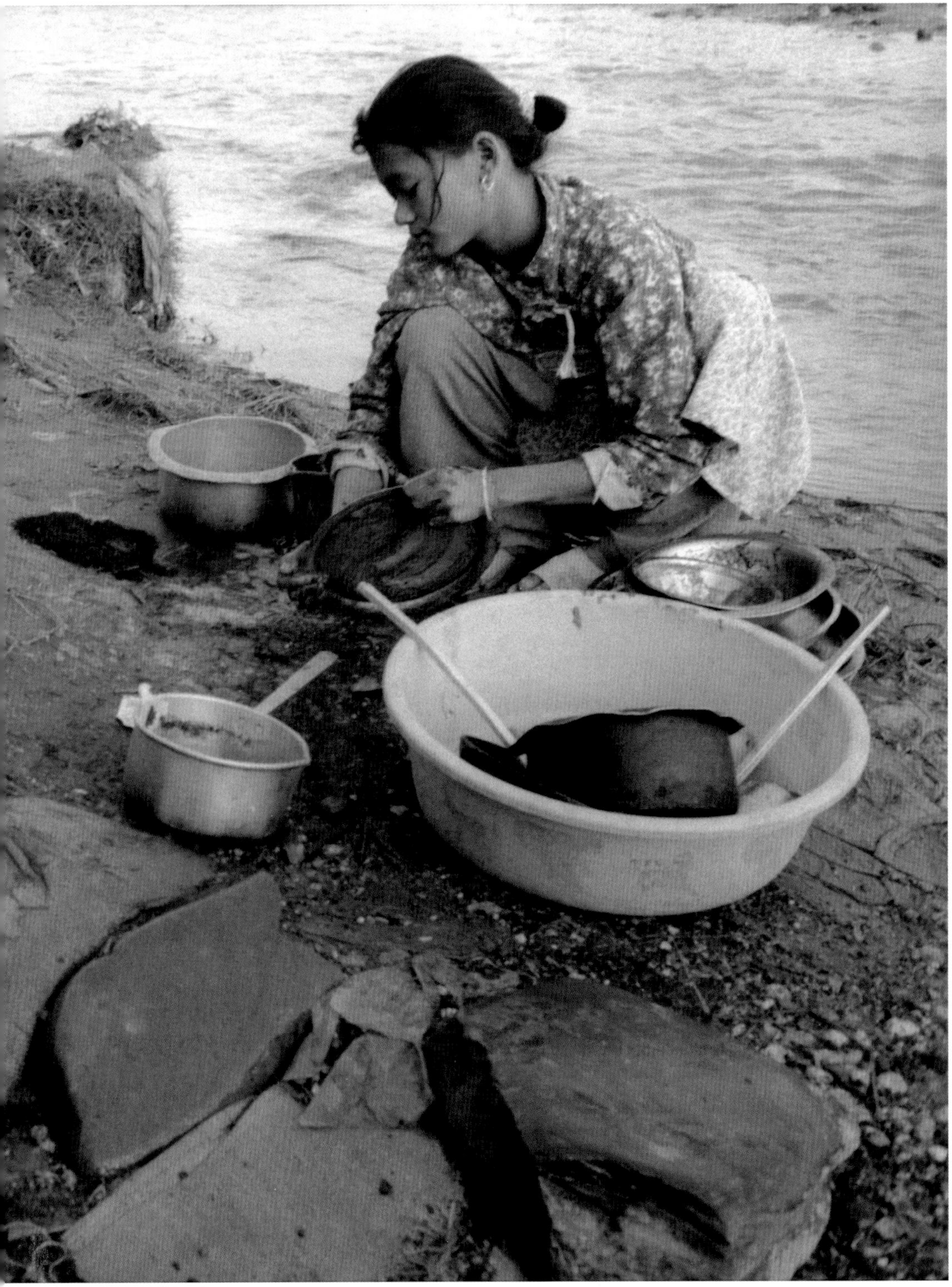

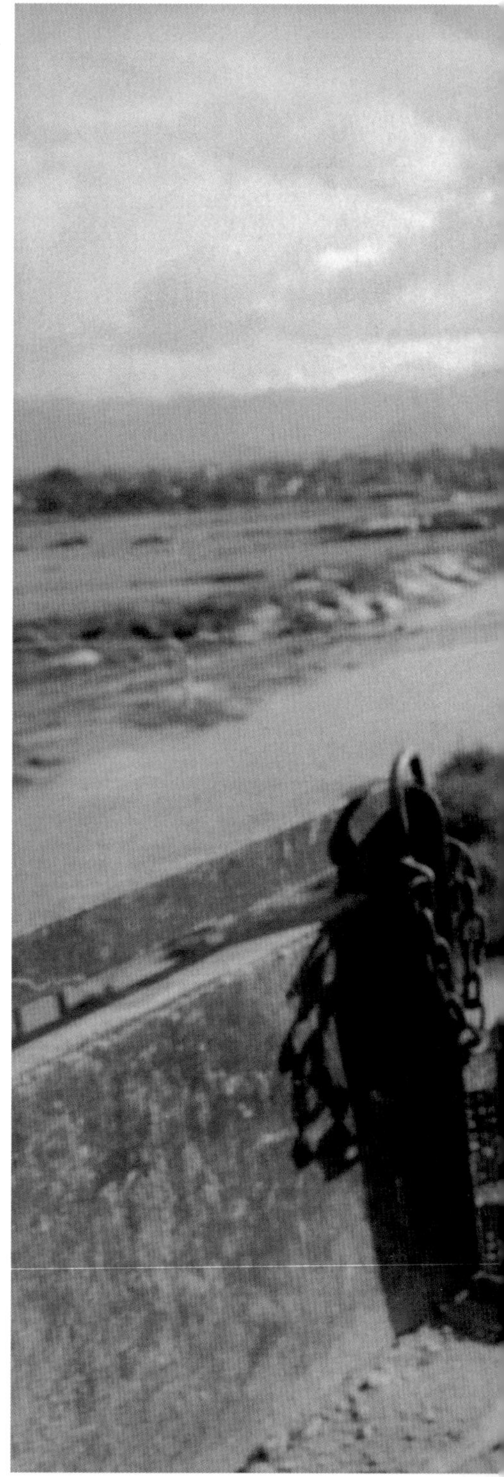

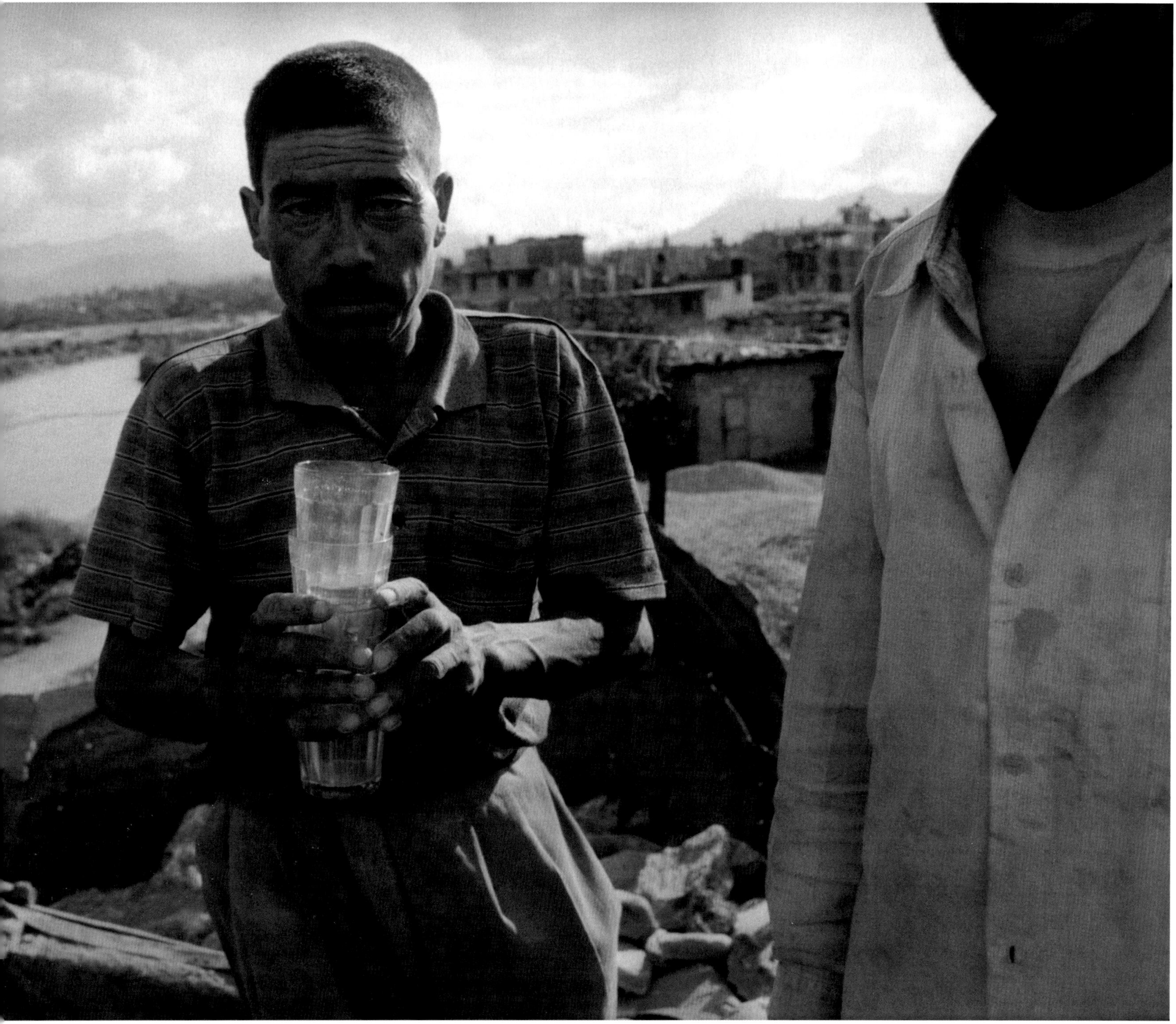

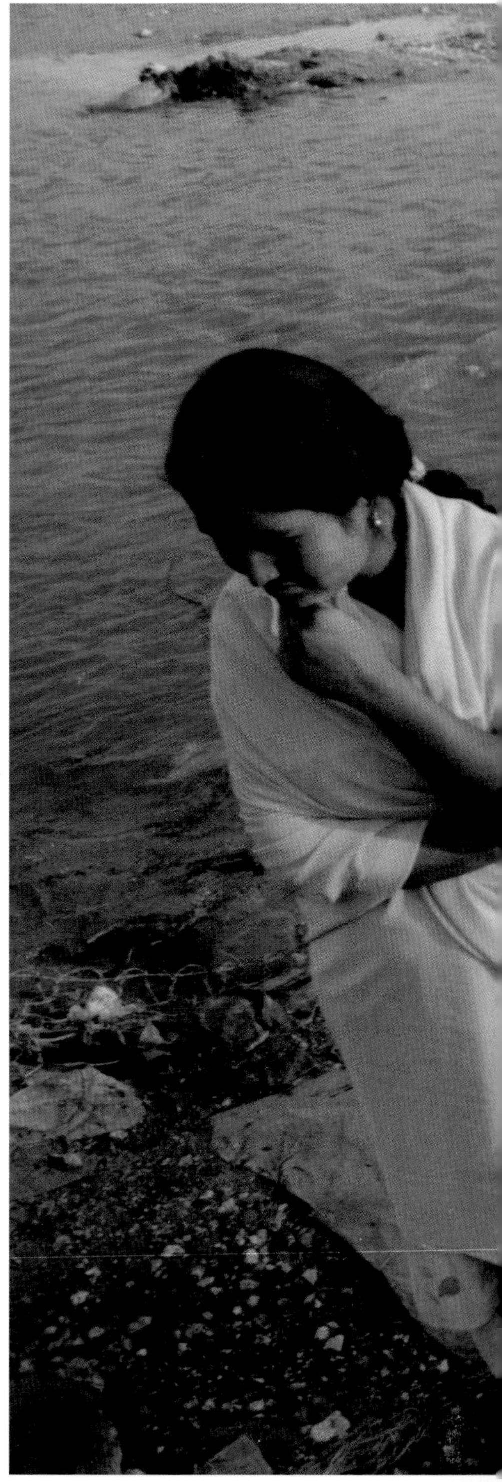

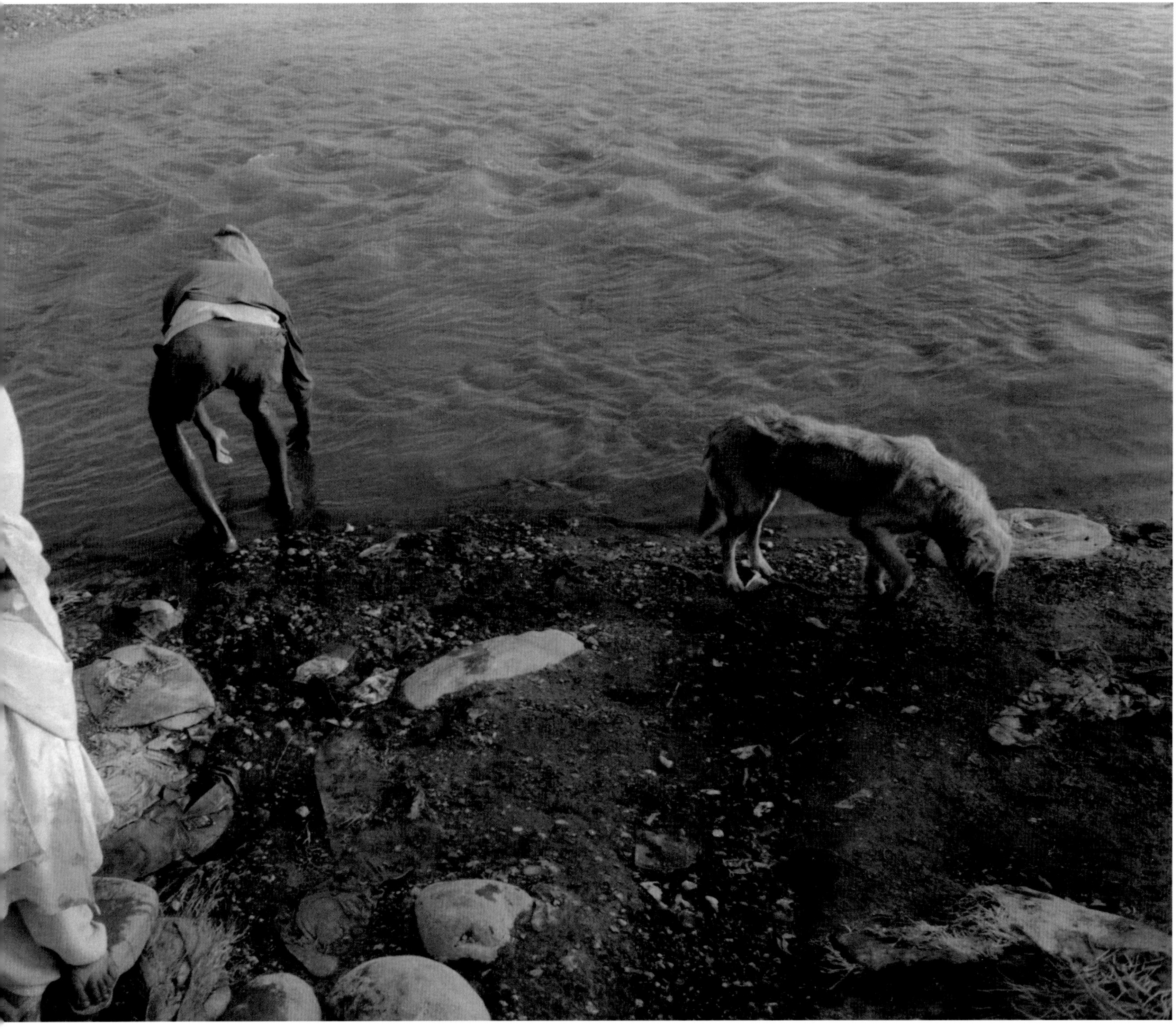

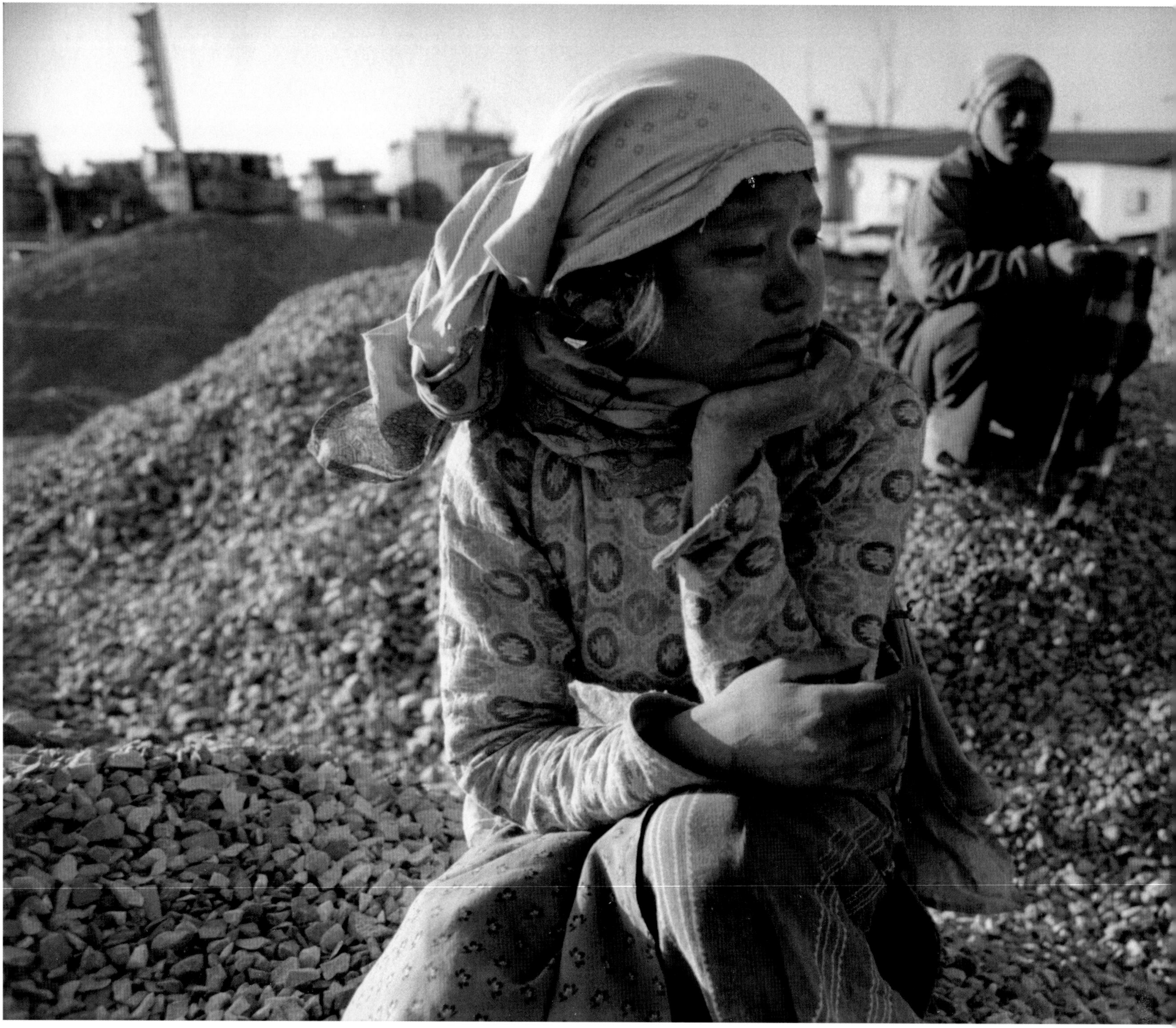

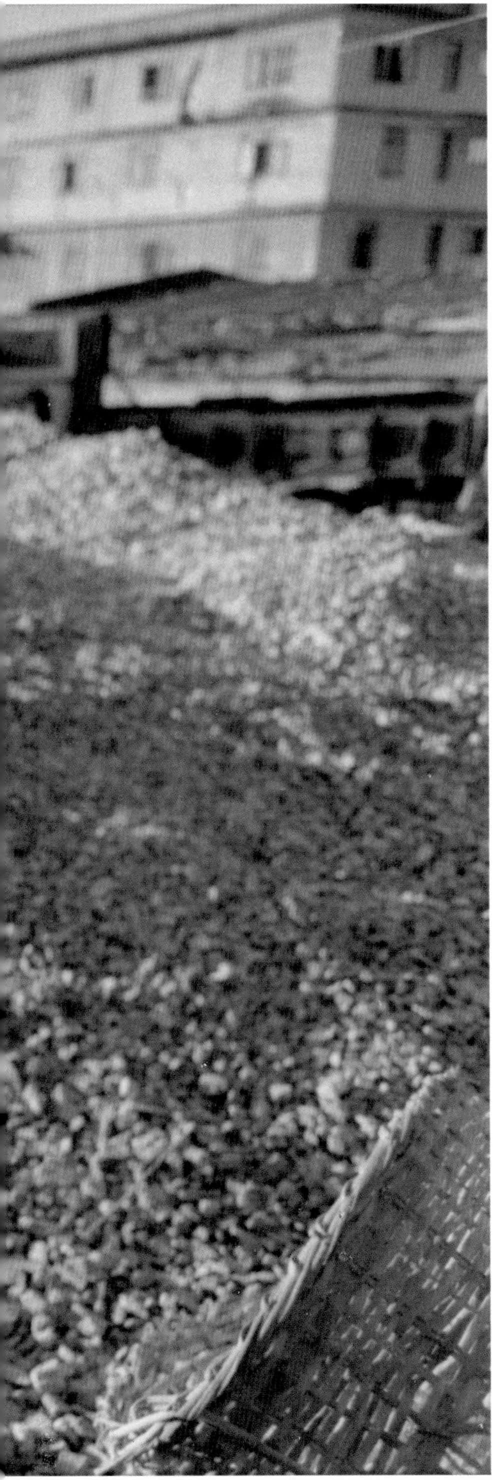

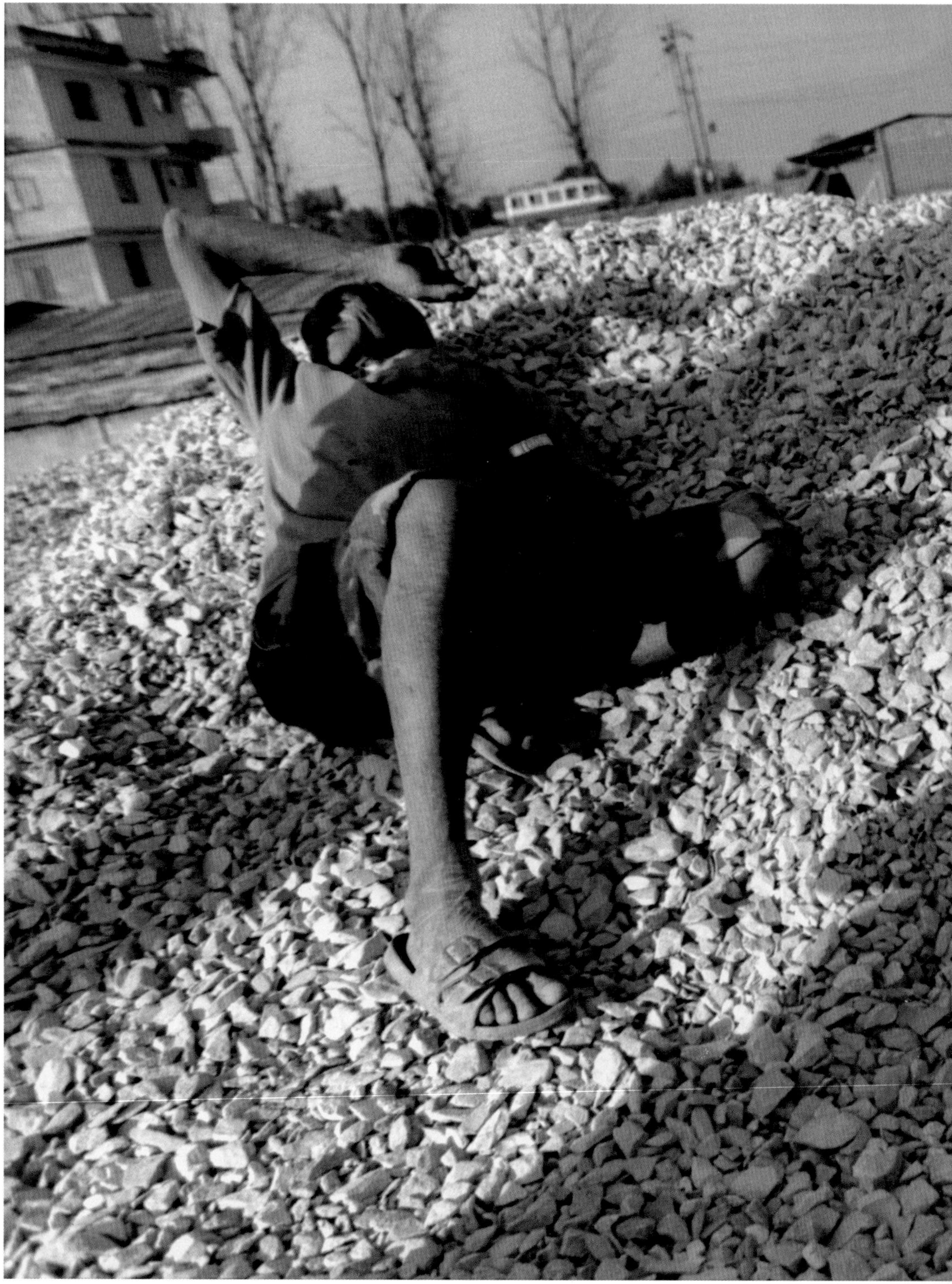

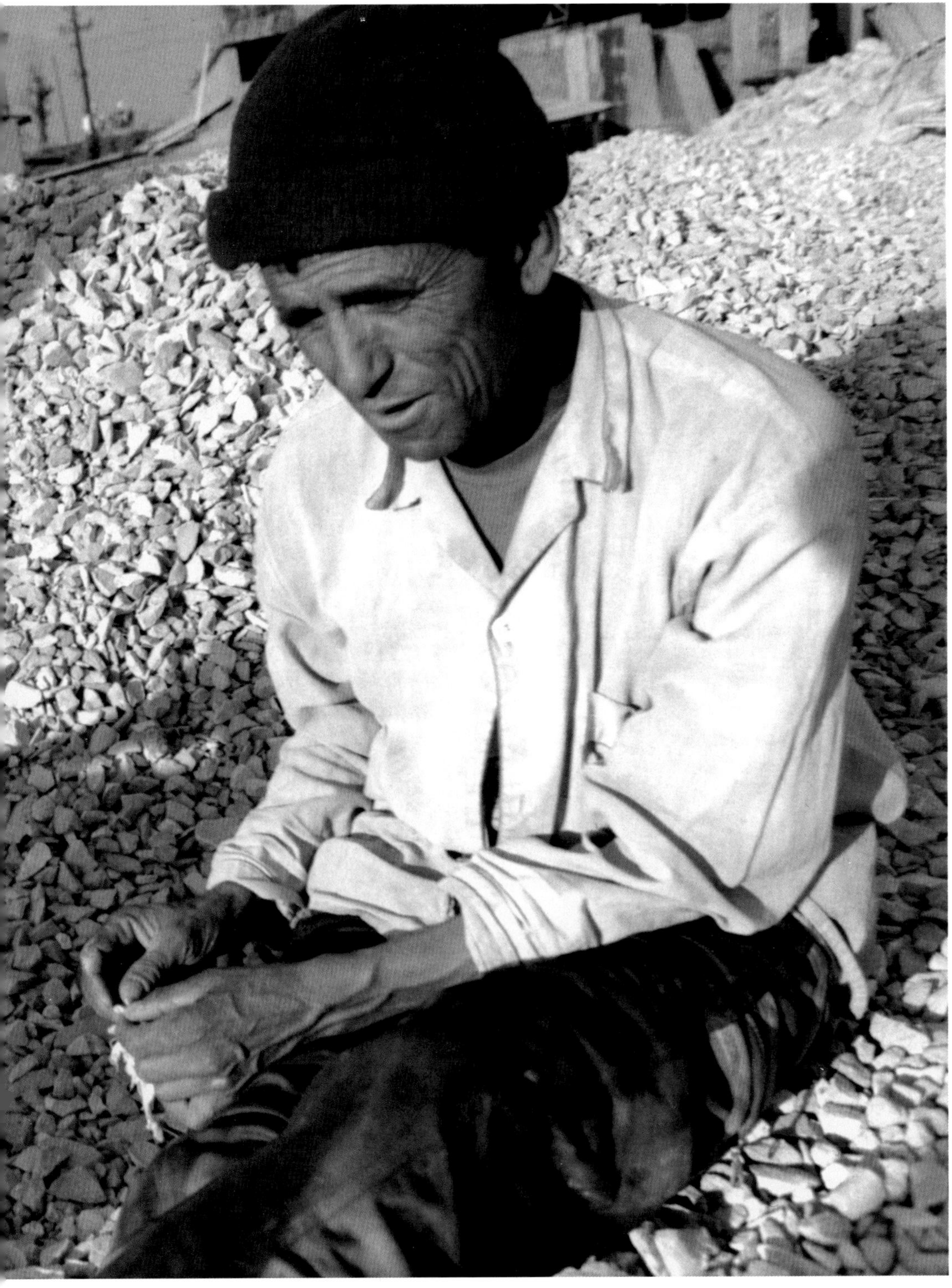

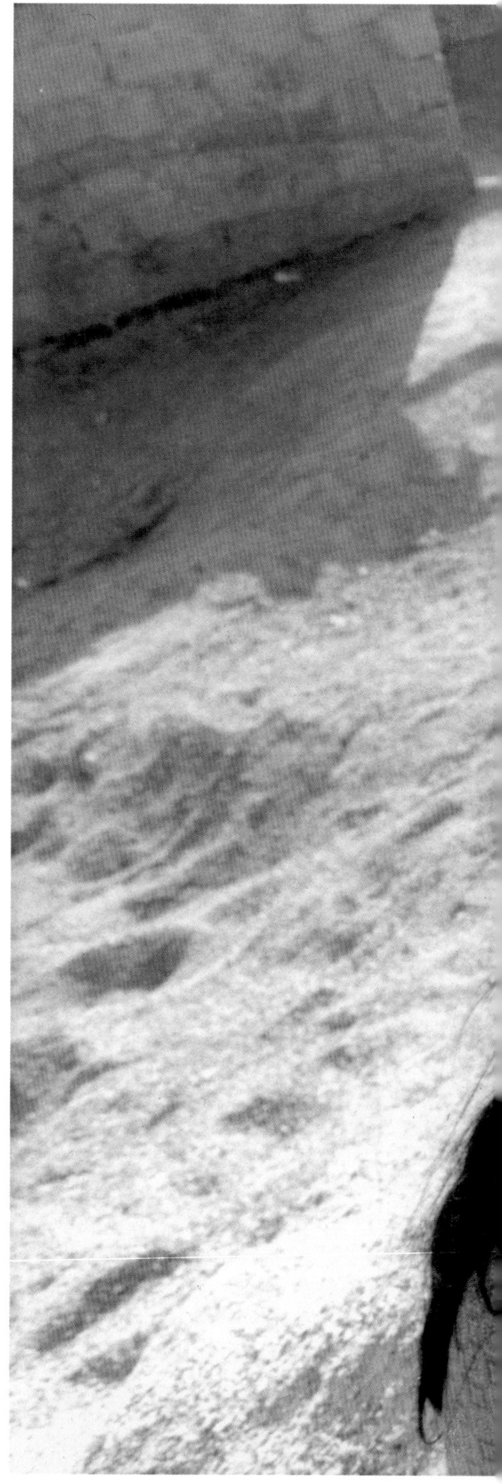

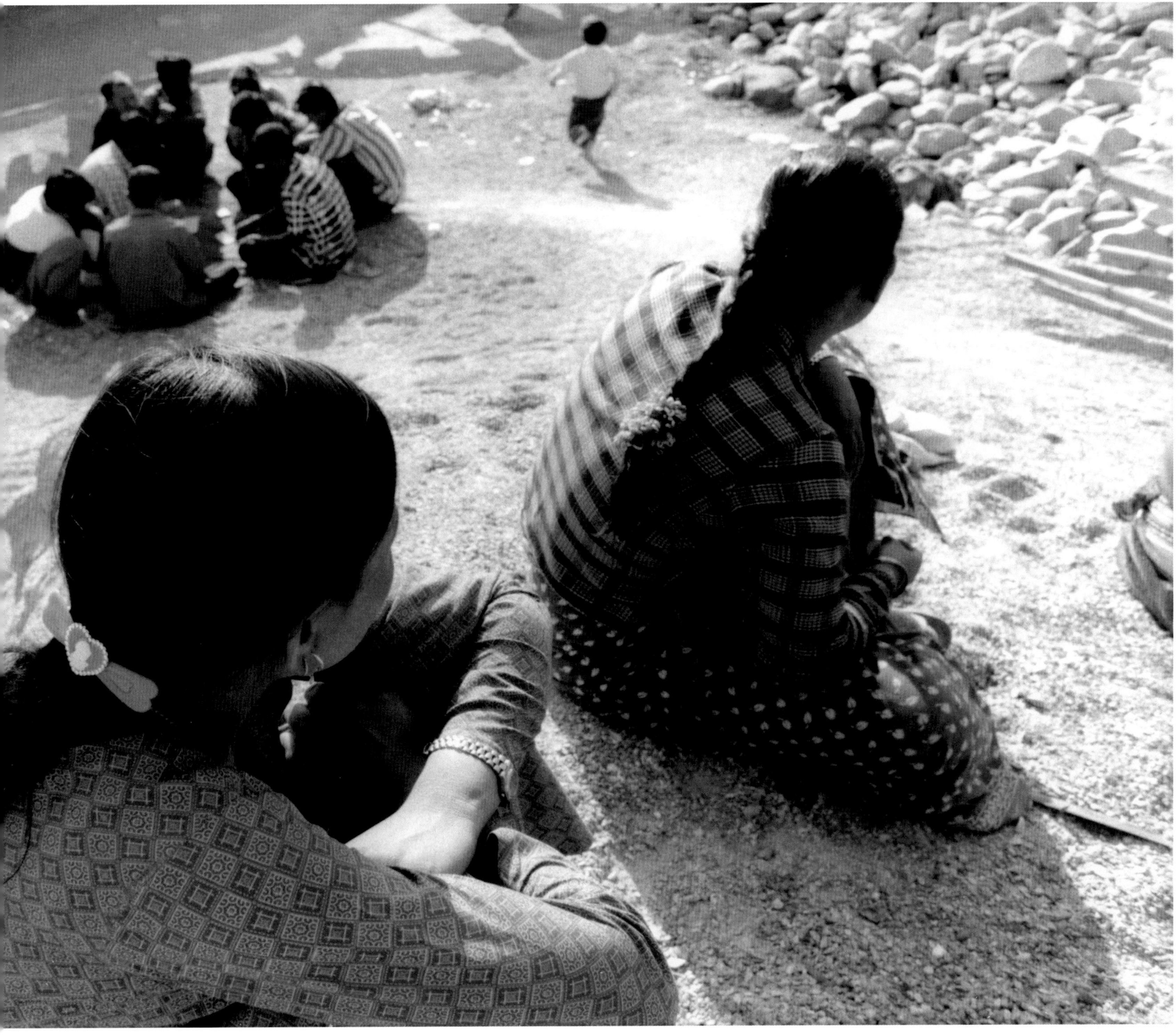

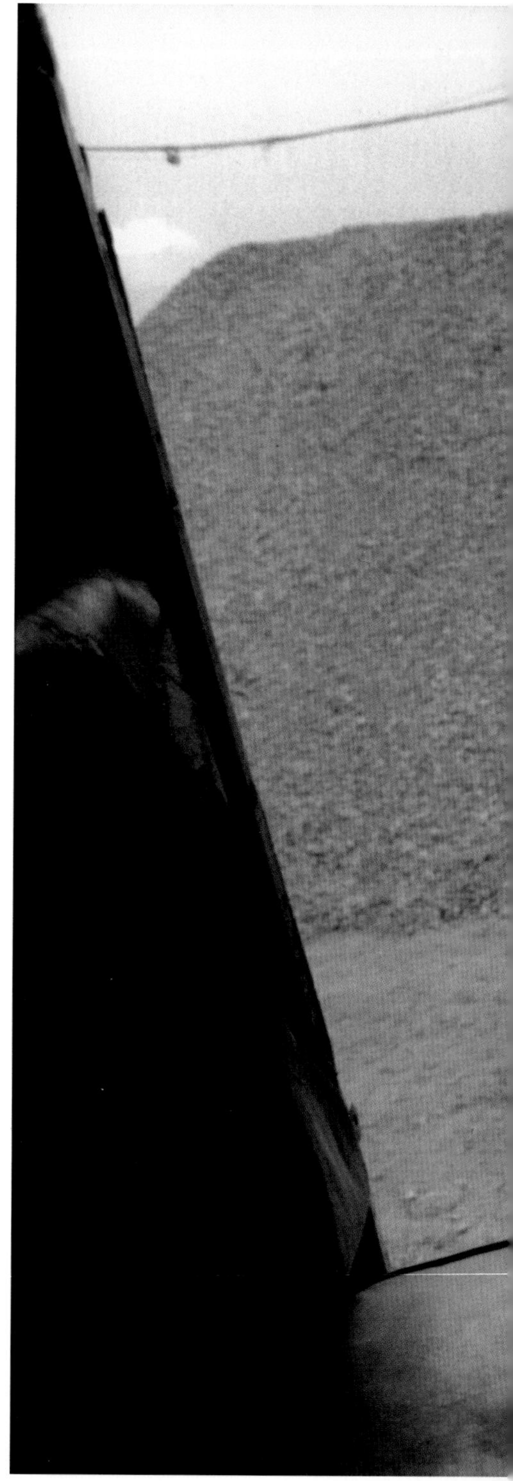

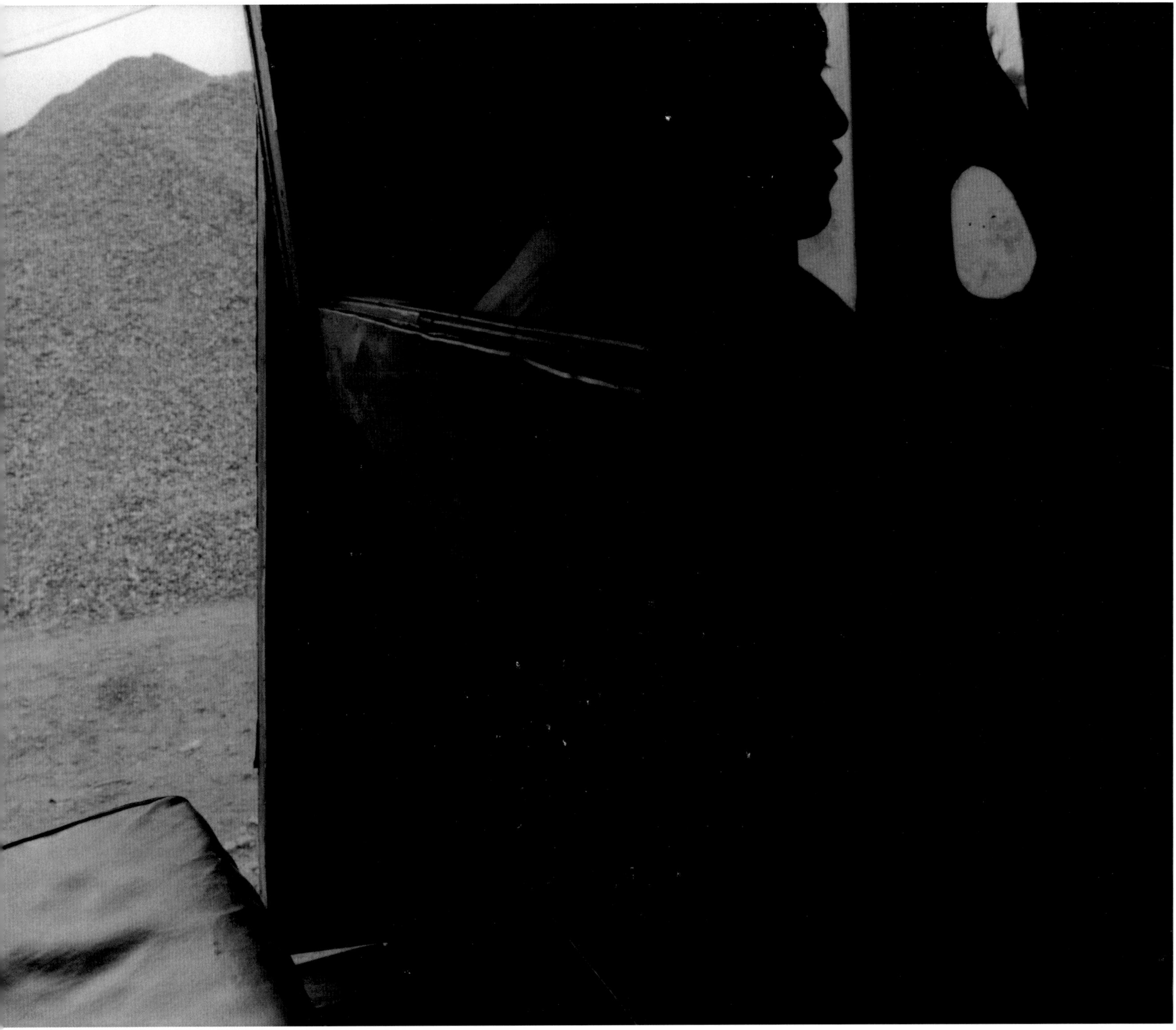

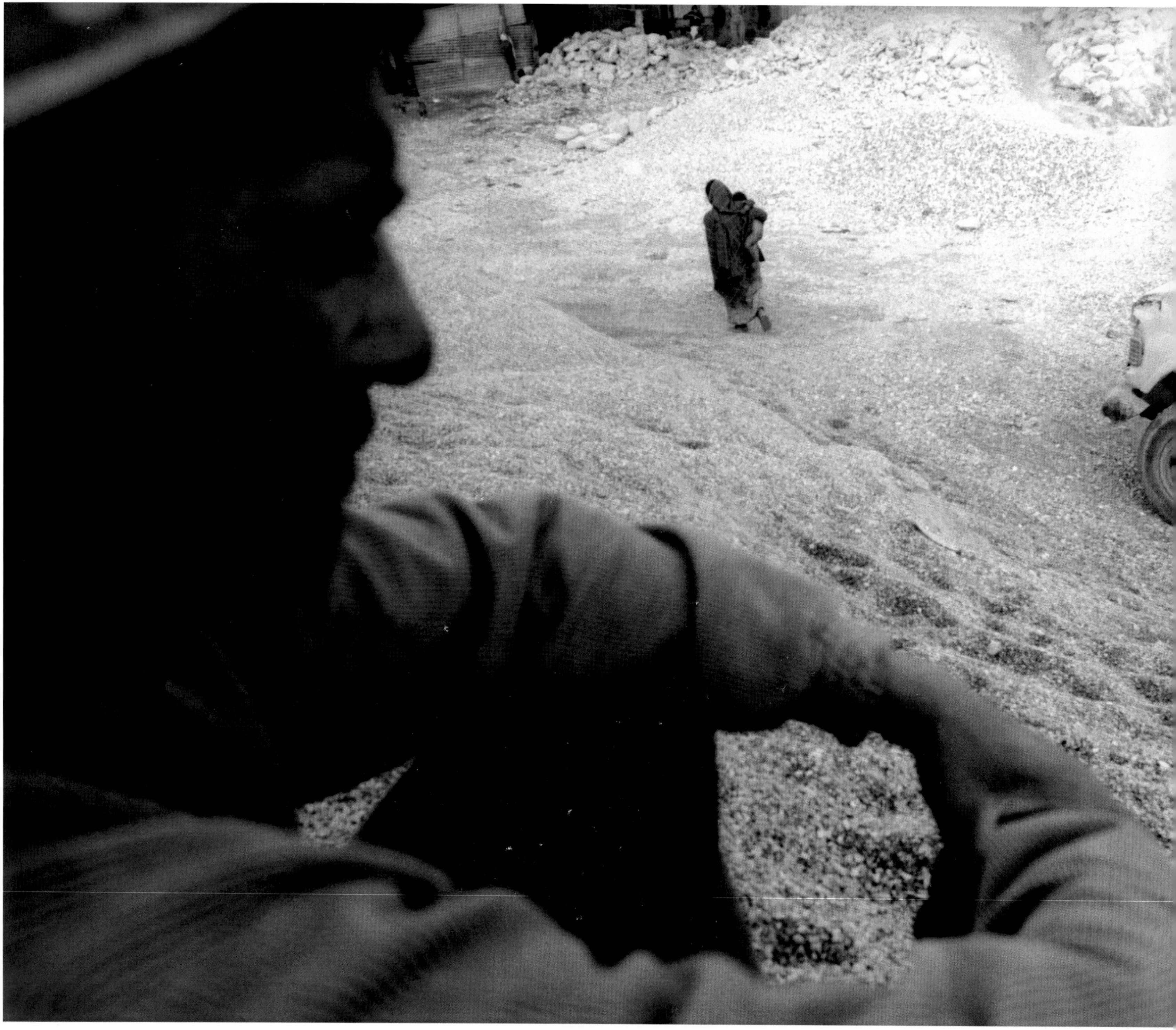

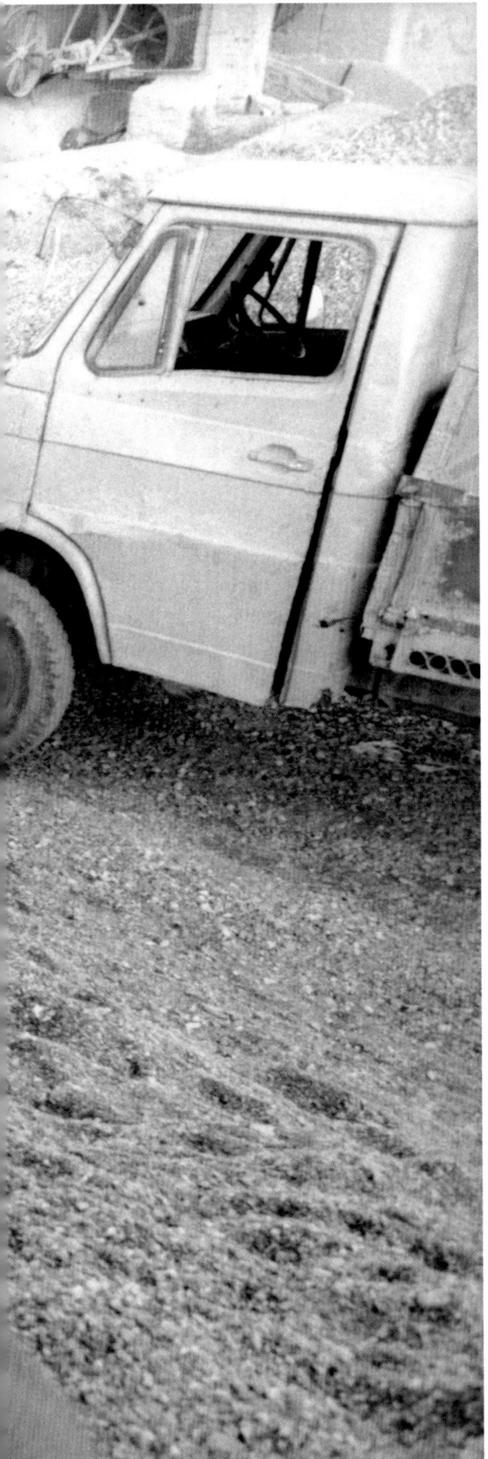

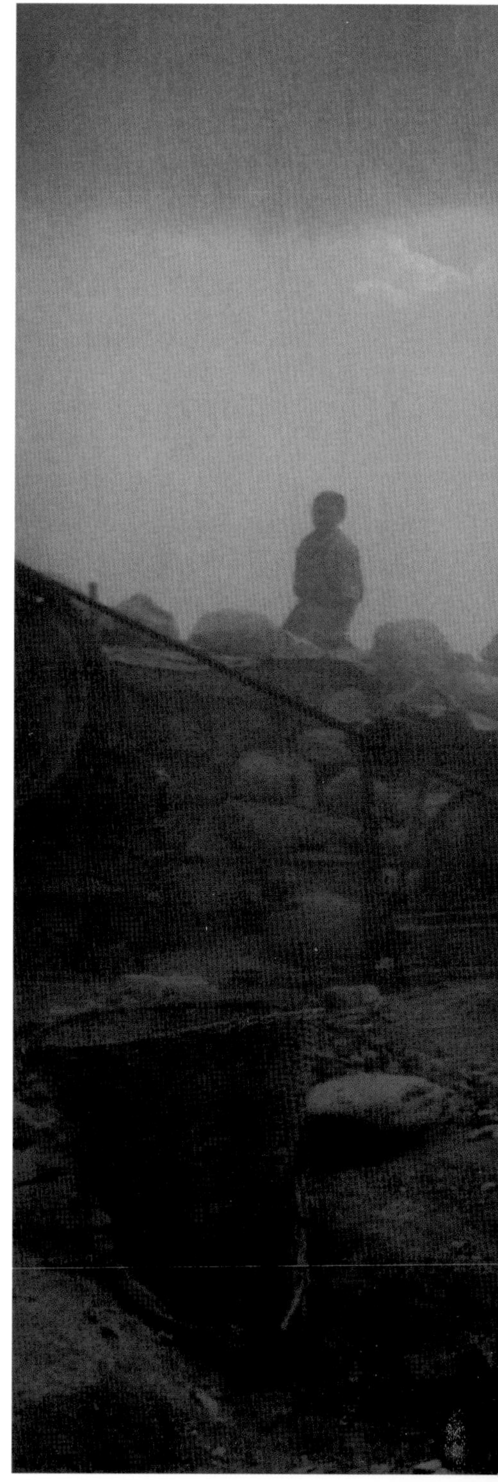

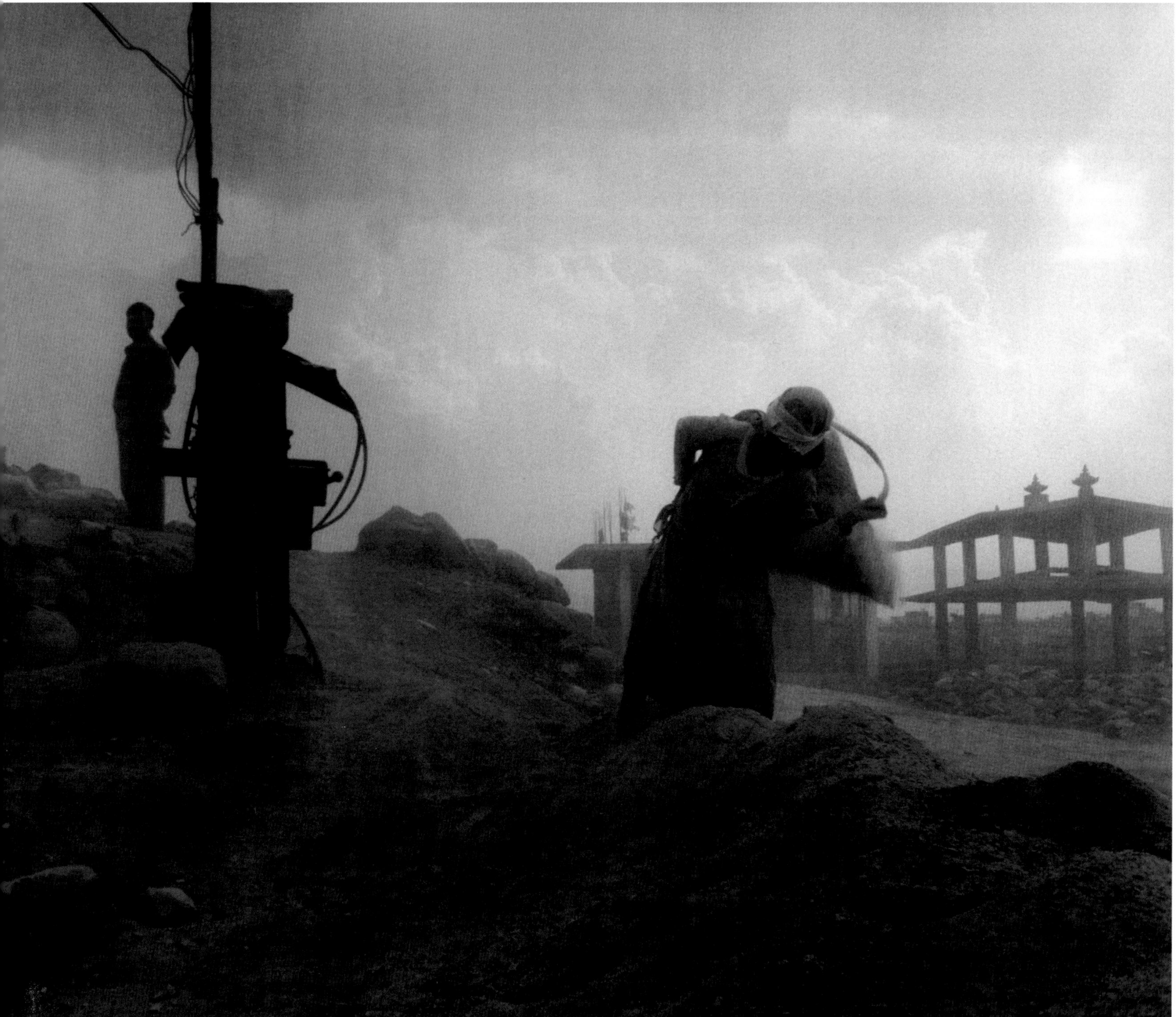

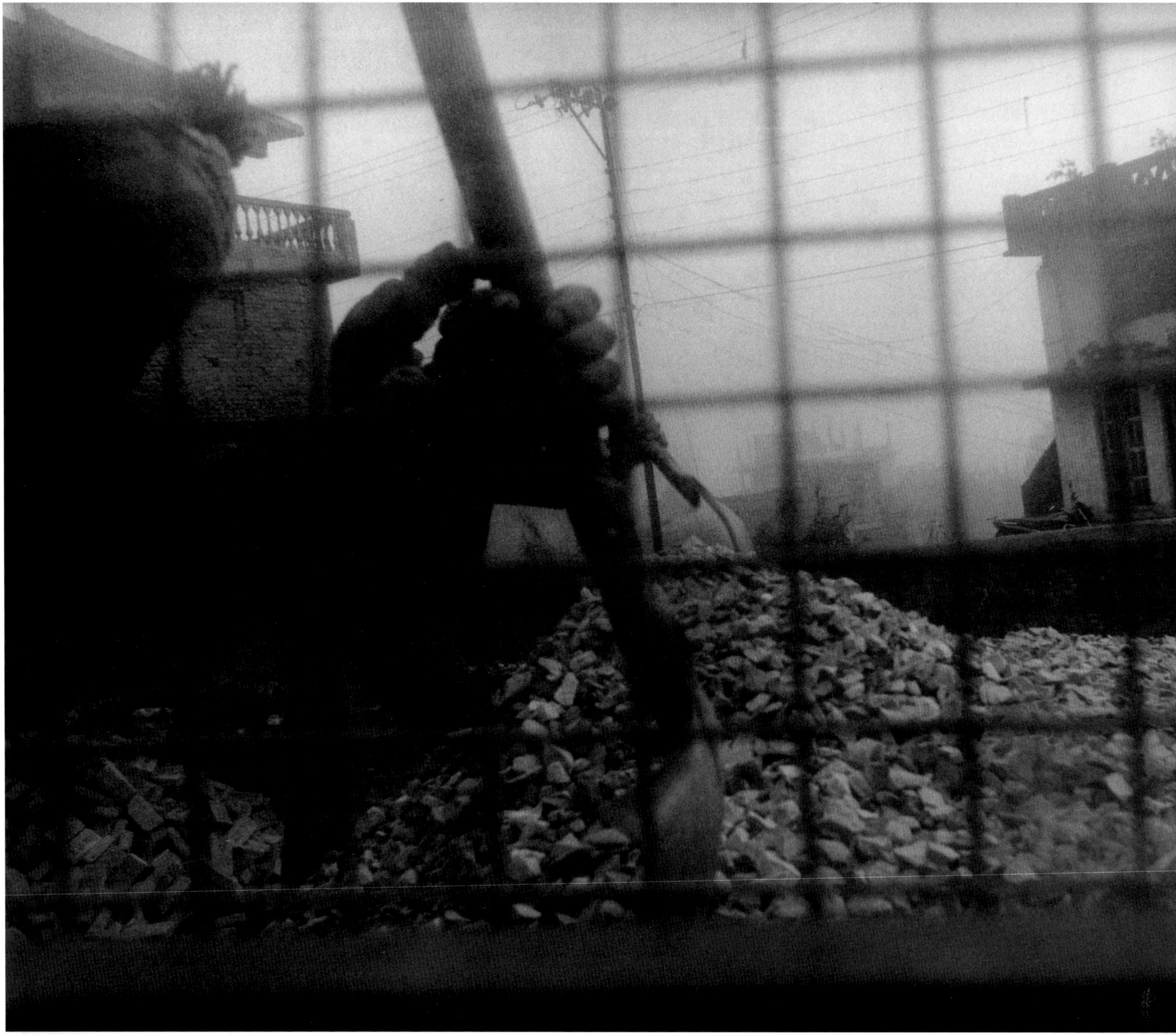

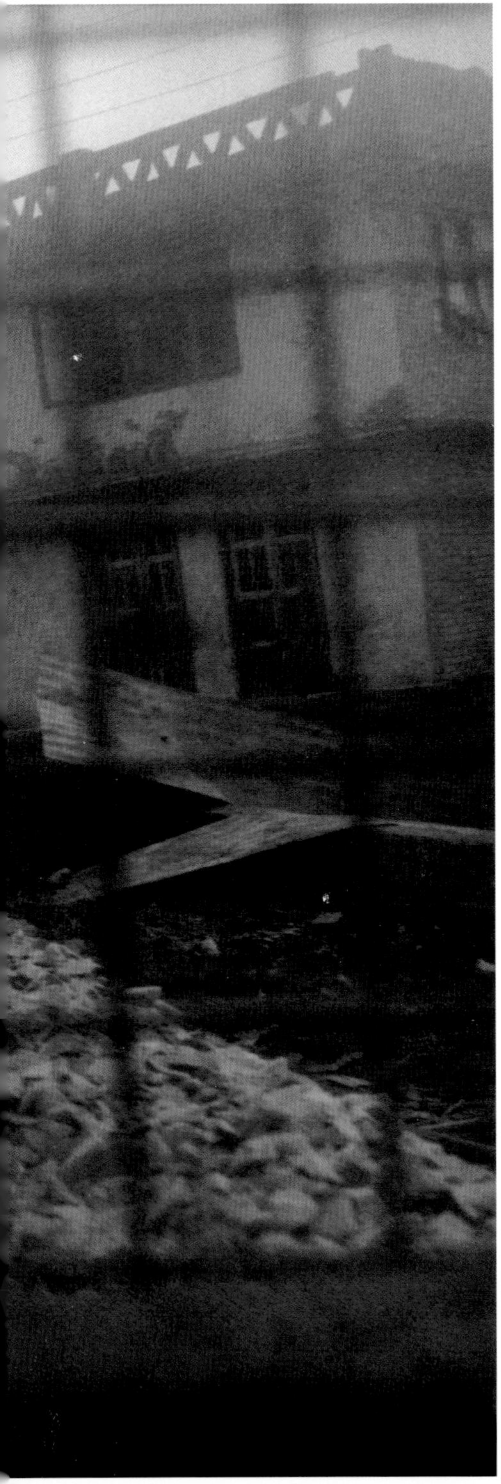

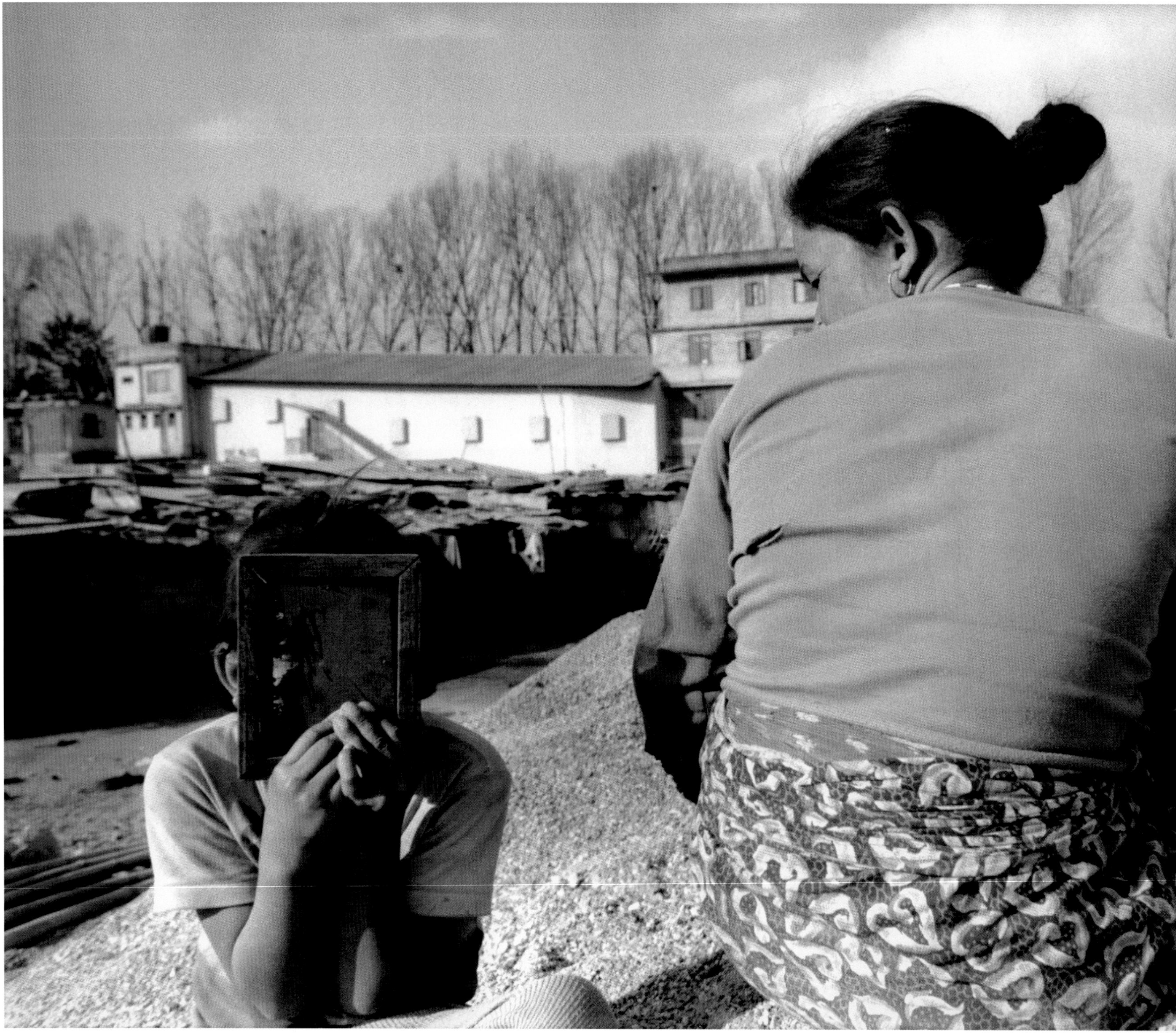

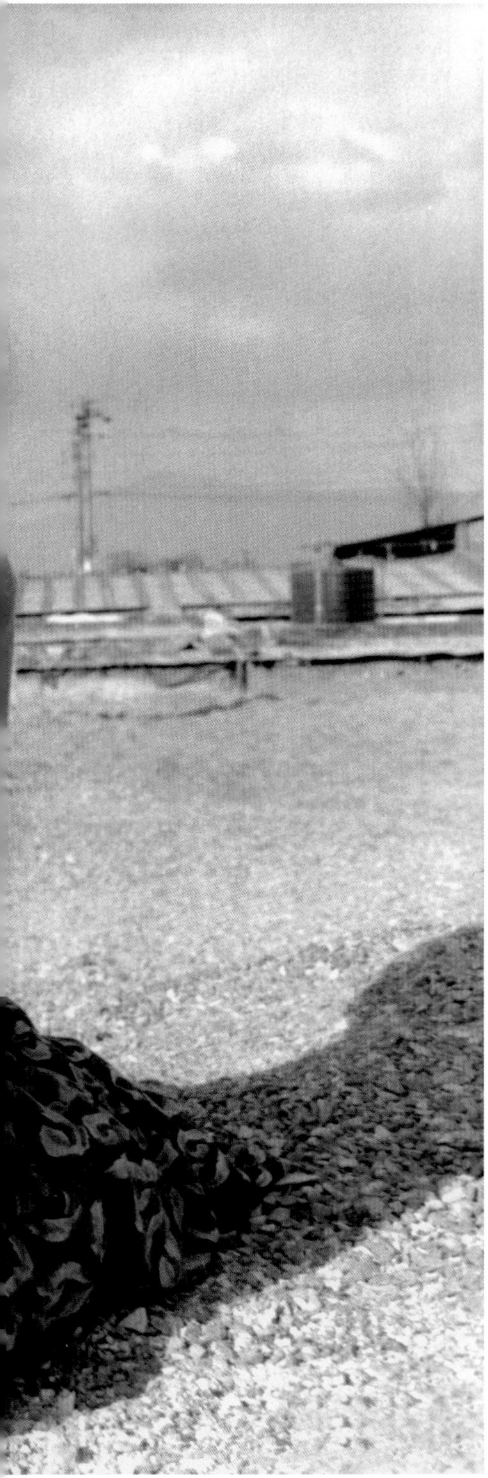

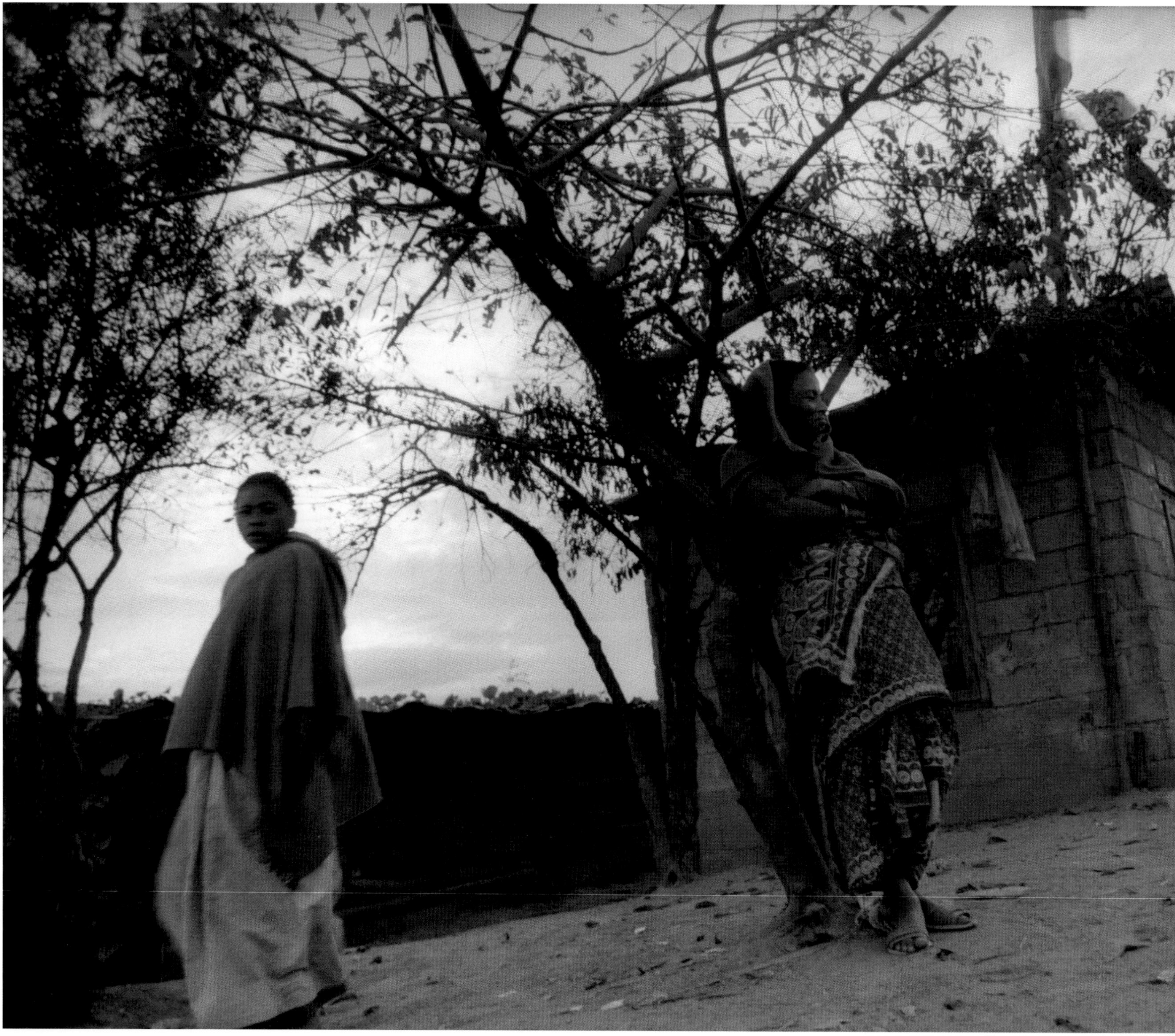

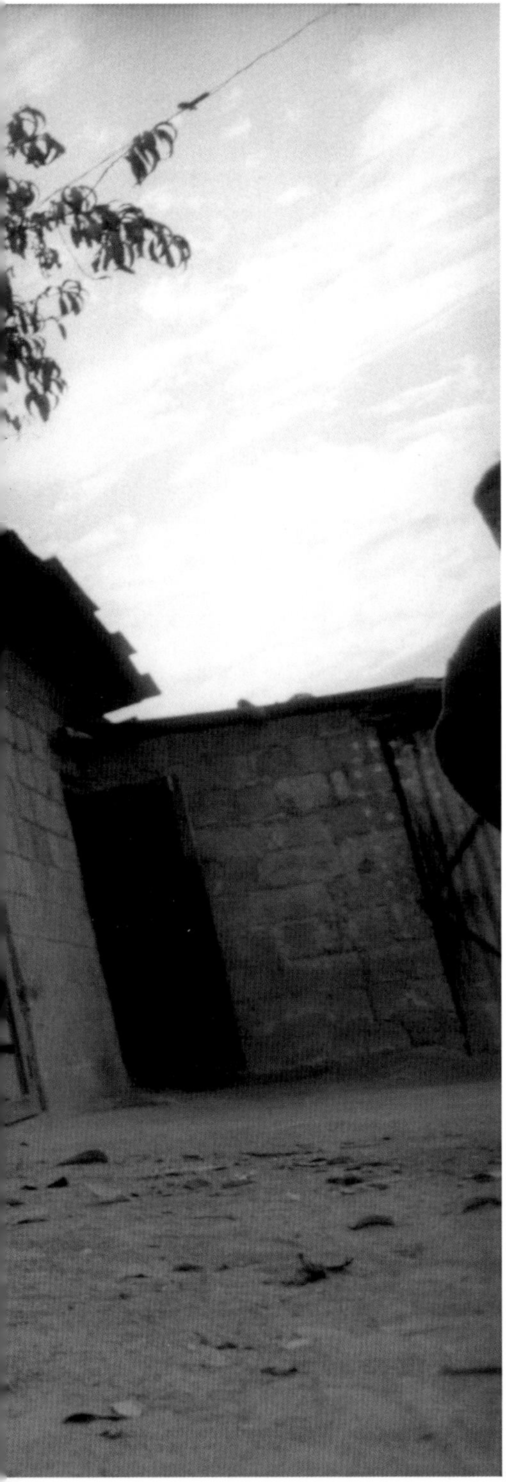

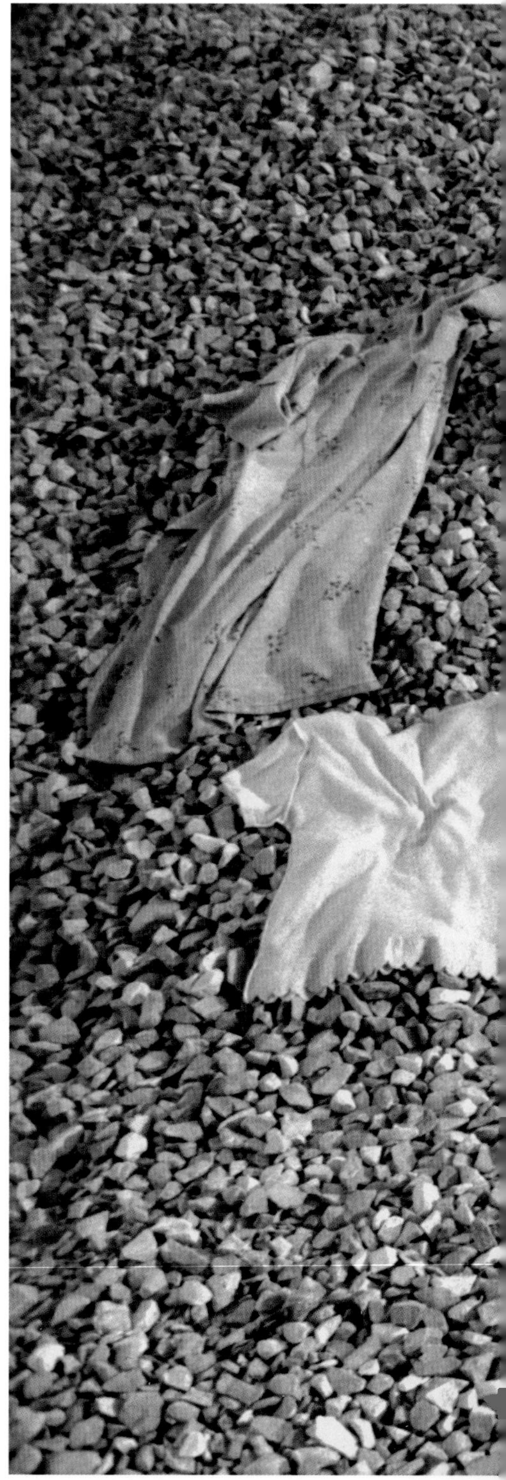

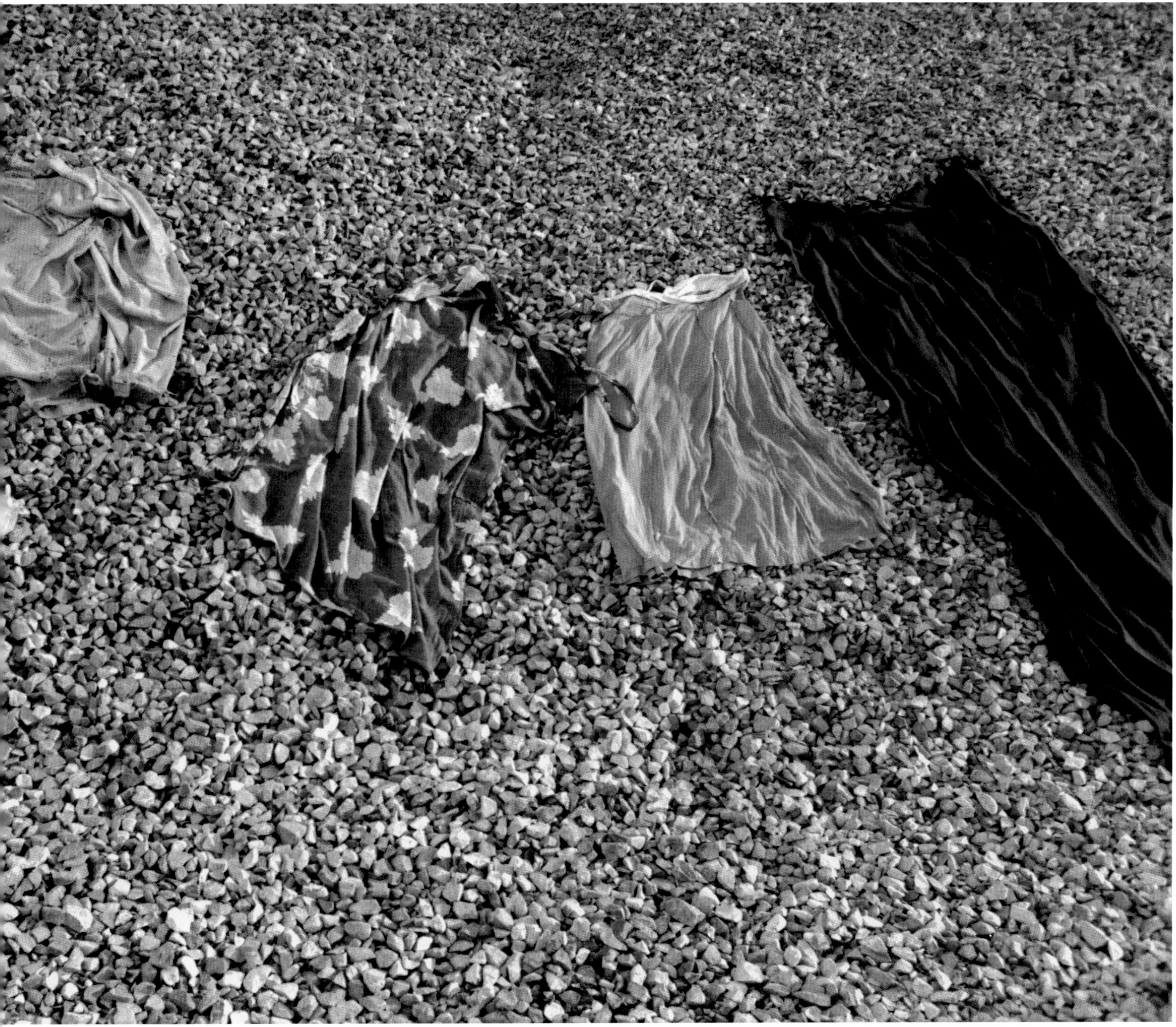

This book is dedicated to Elena, my parents and my sister, with love and gratitude.

Thanks to
Elena Zikova, Gunilla Jarlbro, Bertil Jarlbro, Hanna Jarlbro,
Mrigendra Joshi, Raju Thakuri, Narayan Prajapati, Edward Longmire,
Nick Miseur, Sebastian Sardi, Roman Baigouzov
and workers at the Stonefactory for letting me photograph them trough out the years.

Olof Jarlbro/ Stonefactory
Text: Olof Jarlbro
Translation French: Nick Miseur
Translation Czech: Elena Zikova
Graphic design: Olof Jarlbro, Roman Baigouzov
Printed by Tiskárna PROTISK s.r.o., České Budějovice
Published by Rough dog press 2009

ISBN 978-80-254-4384-2